D0721742

The Teacher's Gradebook

Strategies for Student Success

Barry S. Raebeck

A SCARECROWEDUCATION BOOK

The Scarecrow Press, Inc.
Lanham, Maryland, and London
2002

A SCARECROWEDUCATION BOOK

Published in the United States of America
by Scarecrow Press, Inc.
A Member of the Rowman & Littlefield Publishing Group
4720 Boston Way, Lanham, Maryland 20706
www.scaroweducation.com

4 Pleydell Gardens, Folkestone
Kent CT20 2DN, England

Copyright © 2002 by Barry S. Raebeck

All rights reserved. No part of this publication may be reproduced, stored in a retrieval system, or transmitted in any form or by any means, electronic, mechanical, photocopying, recording, or otherwise, without the prior permission of the publisher.

British Library Cataloguing in Publication Information Available

Library of Congress Cataloging-in-Publication Data

Raebeck, Barry.
  The teacher's gradebook : strategies for student success / Barry S. Raebeck.
    p. cm.
"A ScarecrowEducation book."
Includes bibliographical references and index.
  ISBN 0-8108-4279-3 (pbk. : alk. paper)
  1. Grading and marking (Students)—Handbooks, manuals, etc. 2. School reports—Handbooks, manuals, etc. I. Title.

LB3060.37 .R34 2002
372.27'2—dc21   2002019809

♾™ The paper used in this publication meets the minimum requirements of American National Standard for Information Sciences—Permanence of Paper for Printed Library Materials, ANSI/NISO Z39.48-1992.
Manufactured in the United States of America.

Contents

Foreword

The greatest development I have undergone intellectually is the development of creativity. Before having Dr. Raebeck as my tenth-grade teacher I never thought of myself as creative in an artistic sense. I was purely oriented toward the analytical world of math and science. Though I still hold a deep interest in those subjects, now, thanks to Dr. Raebeck, I am capable of thinking creatively as well.

It was in tenth grade that I underwent an intellectual revolution of my own in Dr. Raebeck's English class. I realized the superficiality of measuring intelligence in terms of numbers because there were many sides to intelligence. Intelligence, I found, existed within one's capacity to create. Creativity was an essential part of the path to brilliance. Dr. Raebeck did not *teach* anything; rather, he invented a means by which he gave his students a spark of an idea to work upon and let them teach themselves, for creativity is not something that can be learned from others. Creativity is an innate ability that we all have to a certain extent. For most, being creative is just a matter of having the mind properly cultivated.

Each "spark of an idea" that Dr. Raebeck provided me with would blaze up into an utter conflagration. He never imposed a method of thinking upon me. Instead, he let me "explore my mind," so to speak, in a way that I had never had an opportunity to do before. His classes were always quite relaxing. In accordance with Dr. Raebeck's voice, which never seemed to rise far above a whisper, the class was always flooded not with Dr. Raebeck's ideas, but with those ideas of my classmates. The class was organized solely by virtue of intellectual interaction between students and teacher, or even students and students. Often we would hold a "Socratic seminar" in which the entire class sat in a big circle to discuss a literary work. Dr. Raebeck intervened less and less in these seminars as the year progressed.

I found my deepest creative interest to be in our robust poetry unit. Being a poet himself, Dr. Raebeck was the first and only teacher I ever had who dedicated an entire unit to poetry. After reading and memorizing poems and reflecting upon poetic technique, Dr. Raebeck began to hold class outside on the grass whenever the weather was nice. It was there, lying in the sun and reading and discussing poetry, that my mind saw a glimpse of true brilliance—a brilliance that involved a double function of absorption of past ideas and expulsion of new ideas through innovation. Today I write poetry in my leisure time, all because of the influence of that single month in his class.

Kyle Spagnolo
Senior, Southampton High School, Southampton N.Y.
Poet of the year, 2001

1

The Grading Game

Everything we do in education must lead to increased learning and increased interest in further learning. If our processes do not accomplish at least one, and preferably both, of these goals, they are counterproductive. Grading as a regular and sole means of assessing the academic progress of human beings is highly suspect. In my twenty-six years as a professional educator, I have seen little to indicate that grading promotes learning or increases interest. I have seen a great deal of discouragement, anxiety, competitiveness, and confusion resulting from grading, along with some satisfaction on the part of the approximately 10 percent of students who routinely receive the top grades, grades that they feel are appropriate. I worked for a time in an independent school where grades were not given. Not only did I see how little they were missed, I saw no decrease in learning or interest, but rather a marked increase in both.

Grading, however, serves other functions for us. On the plus side, grading allows for measures of accountability. It can prove rewarding to students as positive feedback for work well done. It can provide structure and focus that might otherwise be diminished, and effective grading certainly can prove satisfactory as one means of describing learning success. In the neutral—though at times negative—area, grading enables us to sort and select students, and it provides conformity to established education tradition. As a society we are comfortable with grades. The notion of grading and thus ranking people competitively is deeply ingrained in our culture. Grades will be with us for a while, I suspect.

What I have attempted in writing this book is to provide classroom teachers with fresh perspectives on grading, as well as practical strategies for using the grading process to the advantage of those it is meant to serve—our students. In order to accept this last notion—that grading is meant to serve students and foster their education rather than simply categorize the degree of their learning competency and rank them accordingly or, worse, control and punish them—a few points of philosophy need be explored.

LEARNING FOR LEARNING'S SAKE

This topic may seem quaint, old-fashioned, "Summerhillian," "progressive," or hopelessly out-of-touch in our high-tech, profit-driven, global economy. So many Americans see education as a means to an end. We want to get our tickets punched, move to the next level on the pay scale, max out the next credit card, consume the next all-you-can-eat buffet. But is this totally healthy?

Do children begin this way, fighting off their diaper-clad rivals, clawing their way out of the sandbox to the tricycles, climbing over one another like Yertle the Turtle? Or are children far more altruistic than the dog-eat-doggers would have us believe (Kohn 1990)? Do children need us to evaluate and enumerate everything they do?

What does happen when we criticize the efforts of young children? How soon do they get discouraged? Have you seen a child give up an interest when confronted with adult criticism or the fear of socially imposed failure? The stories are legion, and the facts speak volumes (Glasser 1990; Hannaford 1995; Whitehead 1929). Young children do not respond well to criticism, and frustration quickly leads to abandoning the involvement. This is a truism that needs no further expansion here.

Try teaching a six-year-old to ride a two-wheeler. I have taught three, more or less. This is a frustrating, difficult, tedious, scary, and exhausting task for the parent, let alone the kid! Each child was different in approach, interest, confidence, and capability. Each one took a different time frame, from five sessions in one week to thirty sessions over two years. Each one eventually learned to ride a bike just fine. What is the secret to success there? Choose from the two lists following which adult characteristics might prove more beneficial for such a task.

List A

- Anxiety
- Strong negative words
- Pressure to succeed
- Impatience
- Short time frames with something else looming
- Public criticism
- Unfavorable comparisons to other children
- Quitting the session in head-shaking, muttering obscenity

List B

- Constant verbal reassurance
- Long, uninterrupted time frames
- Patience, patience, patience
- Constant encouragement and belief in eventual success
- Envisioning a positive result
- Enjoying the process
- Gently but firmly persisting through the struggles
- Ending each session on an up note
- Mask of calm despite inner desperation

This may seem simplistic, but parenting and teaching success often depend on our maintaining the energy and thoughtfulness inherent in just this second list of characteristics. Grading students can be done fairly and sensibly, with many of the List B characteristics in place. All too often, however, it feels like a lot of List A traits, to the hapless students trying to guess how to ride this academic bicycle without falling off and ripping up their futures.

This is not about feel-good, everyone-is-wonderful, self-esteem heightening, smiley stickers on crappy work. This is about hard, painstaking, persistent, enlightened teaching/learning relationships built on what we know about human motivation. Success breeds success. As educators we have to provide powerful, genuine opportunities for students to grow and expand their capabilities without ever turning off their intrinsic motivation to make sense of their world and shape it in uniquely important ways. Extrinsic motivation by itself is a poor substitute for intrinsic meaning. Intrinsic motivation benefits remarkably from extrinsic support and validation.

EXTRINSIC AND INTRINSIC MOTIVATION

But let's talk more about this issue of motivation, long a sticking point for educational theorists. To say that human beings are either extrinsically or intrinsically motivated strikes me as silly. We are personal, psychological beings, yet we are also social, environmental beings. Our motivations are infinitely complex. We do have brains, and brains by definition want to learn (Caine and Caine 1997; Sousa 1998). So there is some certain intrinsic motivation for us to look into things. We are drawn to experiences and situations, and we wish to manage them ourselves, yet we also continually respond to those people and conditions around us, so there is some certain extrinsic motivation as well (Goleman 1995). We want to be happy and productive. We want to be with other happy and productive people as well. We want to be doing something intellectually stimulating and invigorating a good bit of the time. We also like rest and repose, and sometimes doing nothing at all feels just great.

In our classrooms educators seek ways to encourage our students' naturally intrinsic motivation to explore and create while also thoroughly developing their ability to relate to socially established, healthy standards of conduct and accomplishment. Consequently we want to enable our students to refine and strengthen the social and academic standards they hold for themselves. A balanced approach to assessment, and the grading that accompanies such, will prove a major asset in developing both our students' intrinsic and extrinsic motivation.

I have seen the balancing act of such methods, complex as it may be, work in countless classrooms with hundreds of students for twenty-six years. I have seen it work with my own children.

The poet, William Blake, said, "Damn braces, bless relaxes" (Snyder 1963). The genuine teacher finds ways to challenge and bless at the same time.

And remember, all three of my girls probably could have, and would have, learned to ride a two-wheeler quite well on their own, with no assistance from me at all, when they were good and ready. What does that inescapable likelihood tell us about our overly serious, damn the torpedoes attitude toward the learning, growing experiences of young children, and older ones as well? Were we taught everything we know, and need to know, by an intentioned adult?

BUILDING *IN* SUCCESS

When I begin a school year with students, whether in a remedial ninth-grade English course or a graduate teaching methods seminar, I state that I believe everyone in the classroom is capable of getting an A in the course. As far as I am concerned they start the course with 100 rather than 0. (There is no more or less logic in either approach, is there?) I also state that if everyone in the classroom performs at the expected level, I have no problem with giving every single student an A.

That does not happen, or at least it has not happened yet, but it is within the realm of possibility in my system. I do not limit success arbitrarily. If you are in my class and you satisfy the criteria for an A, you will get an A. What is more, I am happy with the idea of everyone getting an A, and I am unhappy with the idea of anyone doing badly, or even (perish the thought) failing my course. I take that personally.

It is interesting to note how we think about grades. Isn't it true that teachers who are generally considered the better ones in a school have far higher success rates (read "grades") than those considered the weaker teachers? Isn't it also true that the conflicts over poor grades most often occur with students and their parents and these weaker teachers? Yet at the same time, isn't it true that many of us are slightly uncomfortable with the concept of everyone getting an A? Don't we assume that means that the class is easy, that things are watered down and high grades are being handed out?

When I first taught an honors section of tenth-grade English in another high school, I also served as the department chairperson. The principal and I were reviewing the departmental grades and noting that some teachers had especially high failure rates, with one teacher giving 70 percent of her students grades of C (70–79), D (65–69), or F (below 65), and only 10 percent receiving As (90–100). Even while the principal bemoaned this lack of success under that teacher, she questioned me about what she saw as an unduly high rate of success in my honors classes, with virtually all students receiving As or Bs (80–89).

I paused, looked at her, and asked a simple question: "What grades do you think the honors students *ought* to be receiving?" That stopped her cold, for of course she had no answer. For if the honors students, the most capable and committed students we had, ought not to be getting As and Bs, who should? (That virtually all these students were on the school honor roll and thus were receiving high grades in their other courses further supported my point.)

At the same time, once we sort students by ability we better provide equal opportunity for good grades. If students in lower ability groups do not have genuine opportunity to receive good grades, they are in a double jeopardy situation, with less stimulating learning experiences and lower grades built into the process. Another principal criticized me because a girl in my remedial English class who was reading below grade level (which is why she was in the class) got 93 on her report card, and her mother mentioned it to the principal as something of an oddity. I explained that she was the strongest student in the group, did every assignment well and on time, behaved beautifully, and was making excellent progress. Was I to give her a lower grade because she was a poor reader to begin with? Again, no answer.

This past year every single one of my forty-five students in two tenth-grade honors English classes had a final average of 80 or above. Thirty-two of the students had a final average of 90 or above. In my remedial ninth-grade English class, every student but one had a final average of 80 or above (he had 77), and 25 percent had 90 or above. In my remedial twelfth-grade class every student but one had 80 or above (he had 75), and one had above 90. Only one student received a failing grade for a quarter. Not one student failed for the year. *In my teaching career, only one student has ever failed for the year.* I still think about it, and I still remember his name, although it happened twenty years ago. I suppose you could say that he worked harder at failing than I did at helping him to pass.

When teachers state glibly how high their standards are and consequently how many students they fail, I wince. Because, you see, our standards are actually quite low if after years of teaching we cannot figure out how to enable virtually all of our students to master the material assigned. For then we *have* failed our students. Miserably.

A NOTE ON THE BELL CURVE

Many lay people and educators assume that grades ought to be distributed along a bell curve, with most students clustering toward the middle of the range, and equal, decreasingly small, numbers along each end of the spectrum. It is important to recognize, however, that a bell-shaped curve describes random, natural attributes such as weight, height, foot speed, or even IQ, whatever that actually might be.

Education, on the other hand, is an intentional, not random, practice. If we are getting results that simply correspond to random attributes, we are having no impact whatsoever on our students (Bloom 1990). A good and successful high school coach is able to train virtually all athletes to improve on prior performance and random expectations, winding up with highly motivated and effective teams year after year after year. A good teacher is equally successful.

There was a recent article decrying "grade inflation" at Yale, of all places. The article in the *New York Times* claimed that most Yalies were getting As and Bs, unlike the good old days. Of course, no actual data were produced from the 1920s, 1940s, 1960s, or whenever "the good old days" were. My goodness, Yale students are among the most capable, competitive, and committed students in the world. For many of them a B is a disaster. Again, what grades should they be receiving? This concern about grade inflation reflects the belief that the purpose of grading is to sort and select, even at Yale, where the sorting and selecting has already been done by the rigorous admissions process (and alumni contributions!).

A TWO-TIERED SYSTEM

The far greater problem than grade inflation in many public schools is the emergence of a distinct and persistent two-tiered population of academic haves and have-nots. I know of far too many schools (including my own) where the bell curve is inverted, with plenty of people on the honor roll, few in the middle, and plenty of people failing one or more courses for the year (20–30 percent is plenty, is it not?). I suspect you may have seen this phenomenon as well. What is more, it generally falls along socioeconomic lines, with the middle-class and upper-middle-class students receiving good grades, and the students of poor and working poor families receiving the bad grades. There are also severe racial implications of this phenomenon, when minority students tend to fall into the lower socioeconomic status ranges and are graded as such.

As also reported in the *New York Times* recently, the income gap between the college degree haves and the high school only have-nots is dramatically wide, and it has grown considerably since the 1980s. Persons with a college degree earn on average $20.58 an hour, while those with just a high school diploma earn $11.83. Earnings are now 74 percent higher for the college educated than they are for high school. These are big numbers and big gaps. What is more, despite our efforts to shape high schools to be precollege institutions, the number of people actually graduating from four-year colleges has increased from 17 percent to just 25 percent during the last twenty years, while those having just a high school diploma has fallen only slightly, from 39 percent to a still surprisingly high 34 percent (Uchitelle 2000).

This reality is as deeply disturbing as it is deeply entrenched. What does it say about our public schools, designed to be the great equalizers of opportunity, when so many of our young people leave these schools no better off, and often even worse off psychologically, than when they entered with the hopeful expectations of kindergartners? Again, are we simply preserving a demographic status quo, having little or no impact in thirteen years of expressly intentional professional practices?

Of course we know that higher socioeconomic status students get higher grades and test scores, coming from more supportive and better educated families. Some measure of difference is to be expected. It is far easier teaching clean, well-mannered, well-dressed students who don't hit you up for lunch money.

The wide gulf that currently exists, however, has much to do with our self-fulfilling educational prophecies. It likely has even more to do with our resultant practices and expectations regarding the inherent intellectual abilities of these students than it does with their genuine capacity to grow and learn.

BUILDING *ON* SUCCESS

We want to begin with the expectation that everyone can experience some measure of success in the class. At the same time we want to continually build on whatever successes students are having. I like to give the students an open-ended, creative, multimedia project early in the first quarter. This experience enables them to demonstrate a range of abilities and interests. In addition, I provide a clear set of criteria detailed in a rubric and also provide models of past projects that were particularly successful. I give them two full weeks to put the project together. I also skew the rubric toward success somewhat (more on this in chapter 6). Although few students do not take the opportunity and hand in shoddy work (the truly shoddy work must be redone; see "No Fs: Redoing Unacceptable Work" in chapter 2), most come through with a solid effort and begin the year with an A or high B grade.

Another important technique in this regard is never confusing a diagnostic measure with an assessment measure. If you wish to ascertain what students know in a particular area early in the course, diagnose the heck out of them—but do not grade it. You want the information as a teaching tool, not as an assessment tool, for it does not assess what you and these children have done together—it assesses what happened earlier, or what they remember of it, at any rate. Let us keep returning to the original dictum: *Whatever we do must either increase learning or interest in further learning, and preferably both.*

DEFINITIONS

It helps us when we define more carefully what we are doing in classrooms. "Evaluating," "grading," "assessing," "diagnosing," "checking," "providing feedback," and "recording" are not synonyms. We provide definitions for some of these words following.

- *Evaluating:* weighing the merits of student work based on previous work, others' work, some standard, or combination of these approaches; attaching a symbolic number (0–100), grade (A–F), or evaluative comment ("excellent," "satisfactory," "poor") to student work or report card reflecting its merit.
- *Grading:* equating student productivity with a number or letter grade that is attached to the work.
- *Assessing:* observing and analyzing then assisting a student in seeing the relative merit and accomplishment in a piece of work or performance, generally compared to an established standard or model. Assessment is multifaceted and descriptive.
- *Diagnosing:* determining what a student has learned to date and where strengths and weaknesses in that learning may be. Diagnostic measures may include local and standardized tests, samples of current and prior student work, teacher observation, conferencing with students, parents, previous teachers, and so forth.
- *Checking:* monitoring work in progress, without evaluation or feedback.
- *Providing feedback:* offering insight on student performance in a nonjudgmental manner, with emphasis on description of actual and possible achievement, rather than on evaluation.
- *Recording:* simply noting that work has, or has not, been completed.

Most teachers do all of these things routinely, in greater or lesser amount. These practices are effective to the degree that they are employed thoughtfully and appropriately and so positively influence student interest and achievement.

THE MYTH OF OBJECTIVITY

How each teacher arrives at a grade for each student is a mysterious process generally subject to little or no outside scrutiny. It is wise to recognize that our grading approaches and methods are highly individualized and therefore highly subjective. We seem to forget this salient fact when we assign grades or examine grades assigned by another teacher.

Teacher grading is by definition subjective, not objective. Even though they translate into actual numbers, grades are not hard data because of the idiosyncratic ways in which they are obtained. However, once we see an actual number assigned to a student's project or quarter's performance, we act as though that number has genuine objective value. It has none.

When we accept this truth, we can become more humble, and consequently more realistic, about our grading practices. We must continually examine and reexamine them, always reminding ourselves of the inherent limitation of such a human construct. When we remind ourselves of the essentially subjective nature of the grades we assign, we are far more likely to revise our methods in attempting to adapt more appropriate and effective assessment measures (see "To Test or Not to Test" in chapter 3). The truly professional teacher always wishes to become increasingly adept at all aspects of the task. Understanding the limitations and subjectivity of classroom grading is a necessary step in adjusting it to educational advantage.

A CAVEAT

I believe that grading people is not particularly valuable. I believe that we have to function as effectively as we can within this system. And I believe that if we structure classrooms thoughtfully we can attain high student success and learning rates.

At the same time I do not believe that all children can learn. Neither do I believe that all children can be taught to play tennis. We do better when we insert the word "virtually" into the statement: Virtually all children can learn. I do believe that.

I do not believe that making it hard for students to fail is the same as making it easy for them to get As. I will say this again, because people do not always hear it the first time (we all have our little biases). *I do not believe that making it hard for students to fail is the same as making it easy for them to get As.* An A must mean something. It must mean strong effort *and* high achievement. The last thing we would wish is for schools to simply award high grades to students undeserving of them.

THE ESSENTIALS

The great majority of students in virtually any classroom setting are capable of doing competent work and receiving corresponding grades when given the following:

- tools for the task
- high and clear expectations
- ownership and interest in the process
- freedom from distraction and anxiety
- a teacher who is competent, organized, focused, and fair
- time to engage in learning
- opportunities to make honest mistakes without undue penalty
- a variety of approaches
- a teacher who believes in and cares about (yes, *loves)* the students as uniquely valuable human beings

All we need do, daunting as it may be, is provide that daily dose of patience, hope, and boundless enthusiasm, while holding to endless expectations for the little miracles that spark our students' hearts.

2

Grading Strategies That Work

GRADING AND OVERGRADING

Not only do we overemphasize grades in schools, we overgrade in classrooms. Many teachers feel that we must evaluate virtually everything that students do. The emphasis shifts from the doing to the evaluating.

Alfie Kohn coined the phrase "reward junkies" for children in those schools offering endless external incentives for virtually all schoolwork. These students become extrinsically motivated to the detriment and eventual destruction of their natural curiosity and interest in learning. At some point they will no longer do anything on their own, having lost the inherent excitement in intellectual exploration and accomplishment (Kohn 1993).

This need not be. Modern brain research holds much for us in this regard. The brain loves to learn—in fact it needs to learn to stay healthy. Every time we acquire new information and skills we create new neural pathways in the brain, new synapses that forge connections and build organic intelligence. When we are learning things of meaning to us (and this reliance on meaning cannot be overemphasized) our brains produce electrolytic chemical compounds that make us feel good. We actually flood our own brains and bodies with a sense of well-being when we make new discoveries and have engaging experiences (Jensen 1998; Sylwester 1995).

On the other hand, when we are in situations that have little personal meaning, or worse, threaten us, our brains downshift into a state of anxiety, and we are flooded with noradrenaline, a stressor.

I often remind myself how little I like being evaluated, and just how stressful I would find regular, even daily, evaluation of my efforts by a superior. Then I put myself in my students' place. For one of the first things we forget as a teacher is what it is like to be a student. We ought never forget that.

Five major grades per quarter, or approximately one per two weeks, is certainly ample. Generally speaking, more than one grade per week per subject is excessive. Remember, a student's grades are always multiplied by having many different subjects and teachers. What is more, if we are encouraging students to do quality work, we must provide time for that work. If we are overgrading students, we are constantly breaking the curriculum into little pieces, or breaking larger projects into little bits. When we are overgrading, much of what we are grading is short-term, low-quality, low-interest work.

One of my daughters had a science teacher in middle school whom I will call Mr. Universe. The man was actually a pretty fair teacher, but unfortunately he had fallen in love with computerized grading reports. At open house he said nothing about teaching, students, or curriculum, but rather spent his ten minutes explaining in detail his elaborate system for computing grades to the third decimal place. Emily would get literally dozens of grades every quarter, approximately one per day, and sometimes more! This was overwhelming to her seventh-grade head, as she (and I) had no idea how Mr. Universe's system functioned, only that it functioned ceaselessly. It seemed that Emily and her classmates were graded for what side of the aisle they placed their bookbags in. What, ultimately, was the point?

An additional factor regarding overgrading is that individual students tend to perform at comparable rates throughout a quarter, semester, and year. The grades of these students tend to be repetitive, do they not? So what is the point of filling up a quarter with twenty or more As, (or Bs, Cs, or Ds) when five to ten are sufficient to justify a report card grade? It is interesting to note that art teachers are as capable of quality assessment as anyone, yet they generally have but a handful of grades in any quarter. This has never been an issue, has it? (For those who say that is because art does not matter as much as math, I reply with a question: Are logarithms hanging on your walls at home?)

The same notion of not overgrading applies regarding major and minor tasks. Students, whether stronger or weaker, tend to do minor tasks as well as they do major ones. This is another argument for eliminating minor grades entirely. It is also an argument for eliminating mid-quarter progress reports when we already provide four report cards per year. Four reports to parents is more than adequate. Eight is overkill, and needless busywork for teachers.

So what do we do instead to catalog all the minor tasks which, although clearly less important than major projects or exams, we still expect students to complete?

CHOOSE ONE PIECE, NOT ALL

Much of what students do I simply want to record, rather than evaluate. As an English teacher I learned two things years ago. The first is that students must do a lot of writing to become better writers. The second is that once I decide to assign the requisite amount of student writing to ensure their progress, I must relinquish my need to read and assess all of the students' writing. It is a disparate equation. For over time either I will assign less writing in order to be able to read it all, or I will try to read the necessary amount and so become a hateful blind man, old before my time. Therefore I must employ other strategies. Such strategies prove effective in other disciplines or grade levels as well.

One simple technique is to have students produce several pieces over the course of a unit and then have them select one for which they wish to receive a grade. This is akin to the portfolio process we will discuss later (see chapter 7). If you as teacher are anxious about quality control, you could randomly select one of the pieces. Science teachers can use this technique when grading labs. Art teachers can use it when grading draft pieces. Elementary teachers can use it with a wide range of student work.

CHECKS AND BOXES

Another technique I use constantly is a check-off system for completed work. This works quite well with minor homework assignments and a host of other school tasks. Just place a checkmark next to the student's name in the gradebook. If the student does not hand in the work on time, I place an empty box next to the student's name—not a zero, an empty box. Empty boxes must get filled, and I need to remind certain students of that routinely (more on zeros and completing and redoing work following).

If a piece of work has two components, a draft and final copy, for instance, I place a diagonal slash mark in the gradebook when the first piece comes in, and I complete the X with a second mark when the second piece comes in or the work is finished.

1s, 2s, AND 3s

If I wish to assign value to a minor work for some reason, I will often give it a 1, 2, or 3. I tell students that 1 is comparable to a C, 2 is comparable to a B, and 3 is comparable to an A. But I would reserve actual As, Bs, and Cs (or the correlative number grades) for major grades. This satisfies my students, while providing me with a simple way to evaluate work such as individual poems when we are writing poetry or short, in-class compositions that do not require elaborate assessment (more on this in chapter 3).

WEIGHTING TOWARD MAJOR PRODUCTS

When I figure the grades at quarter's end, I weight the major projects heavily (approximately 60 percent depending on how many we have done) and factor in the minor projects lightly (approximately 20 percent depending again on their importance relative to the number of major projects). Then I figure a final 20 percent for classroom participation, which includes homework completion and quality, along with several other factors of behavior and effort (see "Classroom Participation Grade" in chapter 5). These are standard teacher practices and no great revelation. It is always interesting to see how another teacher compiles grades, and, even more importantly, to learn the teacher's thinking behind that practice.

NO ZEROS: REASSIGNING WORK

Using zeros is perhaps the worst grading mistake we can make. What we do when we give a zero is:

- distort, or even destroy, a student's chance to get a good grade for a quarter
- assign a punishment far worse than the crime
- send a harsh, authoritarian message that erects a barrier between us and our students
- allow the student to not complete a task that we felt was valuable enough to assign in the first place

Giving a zero is the easy way out. The better way is to insist that the work be made up. That box must be filled, pal. I use reminders, in class make-up time while other students are doing something else (such as free reading), and afterschool sessions, both voluntary and assigned. I see the work as late or yet-to-be-completed, rather than not done and not-to-be-completed. Students get used to this expectation early on in the year and become increasingly adept at getting things done on time, or getting things done eventually, as the year progresses.

DEALING WITH LATE WORK

What is more, I do not hammer students who are late with work. I take off 2 to 4 points per day for late work, depending on the size and scope of the project. It is important that there is a deadline and that there is a consequence for not meeting that deadline. With all that today's kids have to manage in terms of school, home, and community, I don't believe that the only lesson I wish to teach them is promptness. Often they have excellent reasons for something being late, and I will make exceptions to the lenient rules I hold. I am more concerned with positively modifying long term patterns of individual students than I am with rigidly applying blanket punishments, especially to those students who are routinely responsible, with an occasional slip-up. Adults slip up too, and we sure appreciate a break when we are given one, either by the principal or that state trooper last Sunday.

NO Fs: REDOING UNACCEPTABLE WORK

Just as giving a zero is the easy way out when work is not done, giving an F is the easy way out when work is not done adequately. When students hand in unacceptable work I call it just that, "Unacceptable," and ask them to resubmit it. When we use rubrics, there is a cut-off score short of F that is denoted Unacceptable and a circled R (Redo) is placed on the paper. If a student receives a score below that, the work, project, or performance must be redone. Now this means that in these circumstances I must regrade that student's work, and that is extra time for me. But it is time well spent. My job, as I see it, is to do everything I can to enable my students to be successful in mastering the content and experience of my course. Insisting that they redo shoddy work is about as important a lesson as I can give them.

Now they do not start out with the possibility of a 100 when they redo work. I tell them 90 is the best they can get, but of course that is a far cry from 60 or 40 or 0. And the other students have never complained when a classmate has been allowed to resubmit a project or paper, as if that were some kind of advantage. What possible advantage is there in having to redo a lengthy and involved task, with a grade penalty already built in?

If I do have another student ask if he or she might redo a project because he or she got a lower grade than he or she would like, I will allow it, but again with 90 as a cap. Every once in a while someone takes me up on the offer. If our goal is to inculcate a sense of quality and accomplishment in our students, allowing, or still better, encouraging them to rework assignments is a big step in achieving that goal.

REMEMBER MASTERY LEARNING?

One of the simplest, most logical, and effective teaching/learning strategies is that of mastery learning. Mastery learning was popular in the 1980s and many teachers incorporated it into their methodology.

The concept is clear, although the application takes effort and imagination. Mastery learning is, essentially, teaching a topic or skill to a group, assessing their learning, and then reteaching those who have not attained the knowledge at a "mastery" level determined by the teacher, perhaps 85–90 percent of the material or thereabouts.

The key to success here is twofold. First, the reteaching to the group that did not attain mastery the first time around must be different from the initial approach. If it did not "take" the first time, why reteach it the same way? (We do this all the time and then wonder why they "don't get it.")

Second, an engaging alternate experience, or "something fun to do," if you prefer less jargon, must be provided to the group that did attain mastery the first time. So three teaching/learning lessons are to be crafted in order to learn one important topic or skill. This sounds daunting, perhaps, and it is challenging, of course. But isn't it less problematic than teaching the same things the same way with little additional success, while other students sit there bored and restless or plunging ahead and leaving the nongraspers in increasing confusion and doubt?

What makes this less difficult for the teacher is that generally the more able and more self-contained students will fall into the first mastery group, and those students who can work independently or perhaps in relatively quiet pairs go to the library or study hall. Thus we are able to work directly with the needier students who require more time and teacher attention for mastery. Selecting several topics each year for mastery learning and designing the three-part lesson will improve teaching effectiveness over time and supply the involved teacher with a raft of engaging and varied lessons within a few years.

The final basic point relating to mastery learning has to do with those students (most likely few) who cannot attain the expected level of mastery even after a second teaching/learning attempt. The class must move on at this point, so we have to treat these students the way we do any who are struggling. We use extra help sessions, individualized homework, additional time for completion, peer assistance, or any of the other tools always available with our slower achievers.

The beauty of mastery learning is that it deals successfully with a persistent classroom problem. For all too often we move ahead to new ground when many students are not sure of the old ground. This is especially true in the teaching of mathematics. At some point it seems virtually every student "loses the thread" that holds his or her comprehension together, and math understanding unravels into anxiety. Sound familiar? Did it happen to you? It did to me in eleventh grade, although I was always an excellent math student until that point and have facility with numbers and enjoy thinking about abstract concepts to this day. Mastery learning, when employed properly and thoughtfully, can provide a means of ensuring that the great majority of students stay with the program throughout the year.

HIGH FLOORS AND HIGH CEILINGS

Permitting students to complete or redo work exemplifies our notion stated earlier that we wish to make it *hard for kids to fail, not easy for them to get As*. Thus the concept of high floors/high ceilings. I have a bias toward success. I want as many of my students in as many of my classes as possible (regardless of ability group) to achieve at a high rate and get a grade reflecting that achievement. At the same time I want as few of my students in as few of my classes as possible (regardless of ability group) to experience failure and defeat. Surely all but the most twisted teachers will subscribe to that ideal. The difference here is that beyond the desire, the more successful teachers intentionally build in constructs designed to help them and their students attain the ideal.

The higher percentage of students experiencing high degrees of success, the better impact the teacher is having on their learning processes. Think about advanced placement scores. The scale is 1–5, with 5 for outstanding, 4 for very good, 3 for good, 2 for adequate, and 1 for poor. Not long ago a buddy of mine who is teaching advanced placement American history for only the second year told me proudly that 77 percent of his students had scored 3 or better on the advanced placement examination. To me that might be comparable to 77 percent of his students receiving 85 percent or better in class. That is good. In an honors class one would hope for those results.

It makes no sense when some other teachers in honors classes think of their students in terms of bell curves, grading them accordingly, parceling out success as if it were water in the Mojave Desert. That population is already a select one. The goal going into the first class ought to be 100 pecent receiving 90 or better. With those higher expectations from the teacher, student results would likely be a lot higher also.

DISCOUNTING WORST GRADE

A technique that responds to the vagaries of human nature and productivity is to allow for one screw-up per quarter. Let students know that you will drop their lowest grade. Why not? This technique, like virtually all of the ones we employ in grading, is completely arbitrary and no more or less scientific or objective than any other teacher practice. It is especially appropriate for teachers who give lots of grades, because its impact is lighter. It may be less appropriate for a teacher who only gives three or four major grades each quarter, as then it might encourage students to tank one project. Because I generally do not give many major grades, I do not use this technique with major grades. What I will do, however, is to let a minor grade or failure to redo (R) go when a struggling student has made a substantial effort to make up several assignments at the end of a quarter. Progress is what we are looking for in this case. Perfection may come later. In my case I still wait longingly.

ELIMINATION OF UNNECESSARY BARRIERS

The final point in this chapter has to do with our mindsets again. If we are allied with our students, rather than in an adversarial relationship, we wish them to succeed, we work with them toward their success. One of the barriers is "I handed this in, I swear I did," when you are equally sure that this little disorganized bugger did no such thing. Teachers handle an awful lot of paper. We pride ourselves on our organizational systems. We do not lose student work.

But what do you do when a basically decent kid pleads that he or she has given you something you have no record of? Rather than get in an argument, I ask them if they have a copy, and nowadays they often do. I let them resubmit the work, based on the time that they say they gave it to me. And, much as I wish otherwise, I know that I am not infallible. This is not the hill I want to die on.

Of course, if over time the same student plays this game too often, I will grow wise to it and ask for a resubmission but also attach a late penalty. *I must always believe that any work I assign is worth doing.* (If it is not, I will concoct new and better assignments next time.) The point is to get the work done, and done well, one way or another. The more barriers I am able to eliminate, the more likely I am to accomplish this essential goal with my students.

MORE ON ENSURING COMPLETION OF STUDENT WORK

Much of the difficulty less successful students get into has to do with time management and completing work. Establishing adequate time parameters for assignments is one factor in increasing student completion rates. Being flexible with deadlines is another. Not placing undue emphasis on homework is yet another (see chapter 4). Again, we must continually remind ourselves of what it was like to be a student. When my entire honors class is pleading for an additional night to finish a paper because they have three tests tomorrow, what do I possibly lose by saying, "Sure, take another night"?

Go on a little field trip some time and make a few home visits to the houses of some of your less successful students. See for yourself what circumstances these young people deal with. So many of the accoutrements of success that we assume for our own children—quiet time to study, a comfortable room or private place of their own, adult support, nutritious meals, regular bedtimes, books and pencils and computers, adequate lighting and heat, emotional calm—may not exist for these kids. They accomplish what they do despite their environment, not because of it, unlike the more fortunate children we know.

Using incompletes, and using them flexibly, is another aid in this crucial area of completing work. For me the incomplete is just the empty box. Although I take off points daily for overdue major projects, I am much less concerned with exactly when a minor project is done, only that it is done. The end of the quarter serves as the deadline here.

Our school has a policy that allows for a student to be given a grade of Incomplete. It must be made up within two weeks, or it automatically becomes 55. Generally this also works, as students take the time and do the work, knowing that in my class they will likely receive a substantially better grade than 55 if they complete the work to the best of their ability.

I also reward students for handing in major projects on time, giving them partial rubric points for that within a category such as: "Handed in on time, proper length, observes parameters of the assignment" (more on this in chapter 6).

A final intangible here that possibly has as much effect as any number of my strategies is the relationship I cultivate with my students. They know after a short time that I like what I do, attempt to make the experience as varied and engaging as possible, enjoy their company, respect them as individuals, and care about their success. With this awareness as a base, my students are far more likely to behave in positive, constructive ways that will ensure their success. Getting things in on time becomes a requisite piece in the attainment of mutually satisfactory goals.

3

Tests, Quizzes, and Major Projects

THE PURPOSE OF TESTS

One of our foremost challenges as teachers is to determine what information students are responsible for learning and remembering. The argument could be made that students have not actually learned something if they do not remember it over time. A problem here, of course, is that too many teachers have lost the authority to limit the scope of their courses. When teachers have to cover too much material, they lose the ability to get their students to focus on fewer, but more important, things.

A significant flaw in the current standards mania is that state departments of education are generally loath to specify what particular knowledge students ought to be held accountable for. State tests in high content areas such as social studies and science tend to cover an array of often unrelated, and even miscellaneous, information, much of which classroom teachers view as extraneous to core comprehension. Why these august state bodies cannot decide on a smaller list or canon of quite specific concepts, facts, and events for study has long mystified serious classroom educators, students, and parents, all of whom fall prey to a system that refuses to establish clear learning priorities.

Several years ago E. D. Hirsch bravely attempted this focusing and synthesizing of information with his *Cultural Literacy* efforts (Hirsch 1987). In many school districts, however, the educational value of streamlining and prioritizing was buried in the political correctness debate over the items on Hirsch's list. (I do think the list was a bit long.)

The notion of ever actually doing formal curricular subtraction has long been anathema to our educational leaders. Americans have real difficulty throwing anything out, it seems. Thus a nation of cramped attics, cluttered garages, and tag-sale-level curricula.

Just imagine a state department of education informing American history teachers that the focus of the eleventh-grade examination will be these fifty historically significant figures, these twenty concepts, and these thirty events. How much simpler, more effective, and more engaging the teaching of history would become with but one hundred topics of focus in the school year, as opposed to the random thousands now "covered" to little purpose, with virtually no long-term retention by nearly all students. One hundred is still a lot. Think of the benefits if our students emerged from high school actually cognizant of one hundred historical facts, themes, and figures from American history. Ahh . . .

CONSTRUCTING TESTS

When we construct tests we must first admit that our teacher-made tests are not scientific instruments. A genuine standardized test is *valid* (it tests what it purports to), *reliable* (it tests the desired thing over and over again with different students and still obtains accurate results), and *objective* (it can be used effectively by different teachers in different settings). Furthermore, its validity, reliability, and objectivity have all been established over time with a range of students in multiple settings. Local teacher-made tests have not been subjected to any of these standards. This is not to say that local tests do not serve us well or that they cannot be used effectively. We need remember their inherent weaknesses and refrain from becoming overly attached to the results they obtain for us. And we ought to continually refine them based on student performance and feedback.

As with everything we do in our classrooms, we are purposeful in constructing tests, asking ourselves what precisely we expect them to accomplish for our students. Three purposes may guide us here.

The first purpose is to always reinforce the learning of central concepts, facts, and skills already studied in detail. Another purpose is to provide students with opportunities to demonstrate their knowledge in their own words—to show what they know in addition to what *I think* they ought to know. A third purpose is to demonstrate in a controlled setting and limited time frame that students understand fundamental learnings of the course and can show this in a variety of ways.

There is an element of pressure in a testing situation, and that is intentional. In order to maintain a proper level of stimulation (positive emotion) and to avoid descending into stress (negative emotion), we provide students with:

- prior explanation of test formats—*what will happen*
- prior sharing and review of approximate test content—*what they need to know*
- appropriate time, materials, quietness, and protection from interruptions to accomplish the task—*how they will get it done*
- prior sharing of assessment criteria and process—*how they will be graded*

When we think in terms of proper and effective tests as valid assessments of student learning, we ought to keep several additional thoughts in mind.

1. No item on a test should surprise a majority of students.
2. No item on a test should prove unclear or indecipherable.
3. Virtually all students should complete the test on time.
4. Virtually all students should pass.
5. Many students should excel.
6. Virtually all students should complete the test believing it fair and reflective of both their ability and commitment to preparation.

PROVIDING STUDY GUIDES

For major exams I prepare a study guide for the students. All essential topics, facts, themes, and works that will be on the test are noted. If I wish the students to know and remember certain fictional characters, I tell them so. As a result, my tests are not guessing games; they are demonstrations of mastery.

GRADING TESTS PROMPTLY AND FAIRLY

As stated previously, criteria for grading the test should be shared beforehand and also in the test itself. Tests should be corrected and returned to students quickly, as feedback is decreasingly effective over time. One to two days for return is optimal, with one week as the outside limit. Remember how we expect students to turn things in on time. If we want them to value the experience and the learning inherent in receiving professional feedback from us, we need to turn the tests around rapidly.

Another key point has to do with fairness, both real and perceived. If there is a question that many students did not interpret or respond to correctly, and even complained about, that question is probably inappropriate.

I can still remember a graduate school professor whom I'll call Dr. Severity. On a major exam, virtually the entire class marked the wrong response to a multiple choice item; wrong, that is, according to the good doctor. Now please remember that the level of competence and commitment in such a course is invariably high. Professional educators expect to get an A in graduate courses, and they take tests seriously. Several spoke to the confusing nature of the question, and several others noted that nearly everyone got the question wrong. And then one particularly bold, or foolish, soul (who has recently written a book on grading) politely asked Dr. Severity to consider dropping the question and giving the two points.

But the good doctor held his ground. He refused to concede to the assembled wisdom of the lowly graduate students (many of whom were full-time administrators in schools). He believed himself incapable of human error. He even exhibited a hint of rancor for those who dared express concern. Unchanged, the answer remained. And in our eyes the proud and stubborn Dr. Severity continued his semester-long plunge to ignominy, earning little but our lasting disdain. All for two points out of 100.

I have not forgotten that event. When my students cry out as one that I have erred, that a question is obscure or inscrutable, I listen to them. My goal is to teach, to enable them to learn more effectively. It is not to catch, or punish, or prove intellectual superiority. What is lost when I give credit for a poor question? What is gained, in the eyes of my students?

Recently I gave a test, and a section of it offered in one column a random list of characters from fictional works the class had studied to match up with a random list of their attributes in the other column. One of the characters was Iocaste, of *Antigone*, a character of little lasting import who should not have been included. One of the attributes was a poorly worded, needlessly clever play on words ("dyspeptic antagonist" to be precise), which also should not have been included. In the same part of this clearly flawed test, I offered an attribute that two of the characters had ("loves two, loses both" to be precise), although I believed that one more clearly demonstrated it. Many of the students, including several of the stronger ones, mixed things up with these characters and attributes. Nobody had the slightest idea what in Sam Hill a "dyspeptic antagonist" was.

Remembering dear Dr. Severity, I had no choice but to throw those two questions out and reward the few points to all. I then revised the test to eliminate future confusion. I revise all my assessments all the time. It is a bit more work for me, but it is far better than punishing my students for my own mistakes.

TO TEST OR NOT TO TEST

Earlier I discussed the issue of overgrading. This goes hand in hand with overtesting. If students ask why we do not have more tests (I suspect the question is more from curiosity than from hunger), I ask if they feel that there are ample tests in other subjects. They roll their eyes, saying, "Oh, yeah, do we have tests."

"Fine," I reply, "then you really do not need a whole lot more test-taking practice from me, do you?" They tend to agree, with an obvious sense of relief. It is common for the stronger students to have weekly tests in many subjects. I fail to see the point of it. It is not necessary for learning, as students with decent study skills can certainly prepare over longer time periods for less frequent tests and do so all the time. And it takes that much more of our incredibly precious teaching/learning time, which teachers always complain there is not enough of.

One or two tests per subject per quarter is plenty. When multiplied times five, six, or even seven major subjects for today's students, that limited number makes for between five and fourteen tests per quarter, between twenty and fifty-six tests per year. Surely that is more than enough, no matter what the educational goal.

It is interesting to note that in the finest universities in America students are rarely tested more than once or twice per course each semester. No one seems troubled by this woeful undertesting of students at Cornell or Penn State or Texas Southern.

QUIZZES

When designing quizzes we use the same criteria we use for constructing tests. The goal here is to reinforce smaller pieces of learning, not simply load more grades into the gradebook. If quizzes truly are of lesser importance and count less than tests and major project grades, it ought to be clear to students, and to us, just how much they figure into the quarterly summation.

A simple way to keep things separate is to use a different grading format for quizzes than for tests. The use of 1, 2 or 3, as discussed in the previous chapter, is one way to delineate, and thus ensure the proper weighting. Computerized grading programs allow for different weighting, but establishing varied grading formats makes it clearer for students what is a major and what is a minor grade.

Quizzes can be useful when they are focused, limited, and announced in advance. The use of "pop" (unannounced) quizzes is foolish and poor pedagogy. It places undue stress on students and makes learning into a guessing game of what and when. We always want our students to know, as much as possible, what it is they are expected to be responsible for, and how and when we will assess those expectations. We certainly would not want a "pop" evaluation done by our principal, would we?

On the other hand, doing a spot check, or pop quiz that is not graded, or does not count as a grade, is fine. We want the students to keep up and take responsibility for ongoing learning. And we need lots of assessment means to help us determine the efficacy of the teaching/learning to date. Random, unannounced assessments can serve a purpose here. It is when we attach a lasting grade to them that issues of fairness and pedagogical appropriateness arise.

I give routine spelling quizzes in my remedial reading classes, and my students routinely get As and Bs. How is that? That's because (1) the lists are simpler, familiar words, (2) we have an ungraded prequiz several days before, (3) with a twenty-word quiz, I take off three points for a mistake rather than five (breaking federal spelling quiz law in the process), and (4) I offer a three-point bonus word that they have previously had. They look forward to the quizzes, *and* their spelling improves.

MAJOR PROJECTS

Major projects offer students varied and engaging ways of demonstrating mastery and offer teachers varied ways of assessing that. Major projects are just that, major, and they take thought, time, and effort to arrange satisfactorily.

In order for major project work to become a central and valuable part of the curriculum, a great deal of preparation must go into project development and revision. When developing major projects we want to focus on what benefits to student learning are most likely to occur, shaping the assignments accordingly.

We begin with an emphasis on quality. We want every student to produce a piece that he or she can be proud of. One way to ensure quality is to provide clearly established assessment criteria beforehand (see "Time for Quality," the next section of this chapter). Another key factor here is offering students models of prior projects that were exemplary.

For many students the creative act is at first inhibiting, and this tends to become more problematic with age, as we lose our creative abilities from disuse. In most schools today, students take little or no art beyond middle school and often not a whole lot before that. Students, often incredibly creative as young children, come to see themselves as nonartistic, and some will initially be fearful of creating a multimedia project. Those students who take regular art courses will have far less reluctance in crafting such a project. For students, seeing the models—what peers have accomplished in other years—will prove inspiring. It will also enable them to visualize fresh approaches to the task. Consistent encouragement from the teacher, as well as a balanced assessment rubric that rewards nonartistic abilities too, is also required to ensure success.

TIME FOR QUALITY

Time management is another challenge for many students. Periodic reminders serve to keep them cognizant of time parameters and deadlines. The older the students the less we ought to remind them, as self-management is crucial to success in upper high school and beyond. Breaking the project into draft and final pieces can help with student focus as well, depending to some degree on the nature of the project, of course.

As far as project time length goes, that is always somewhat variable. There are a few things to keep in mind. One thing is whether there will be class time provided. If not, then the project is completely independent. If so, however, the teacher has much more control over the process, and students can also work in pairs or other arrangements at times. Major project work lends itself to larger blocks of time, at least fifty to sixty minutes and preferably more. In a forty-two-minute period, not much of value is going to happen, other than research. As a result, more has to happen outside of class. Stronger students with more support and resources at home are going to produce better projects than weaker students with little of either at home. I often provide more class time for the latter and less for the former.

Another factor is the age and experience of the students. The younger the child, the shorter the project framework. For high school students a month may be reasonable, but for elementary it is too long, as those kids cannot adequately conceptualize the time frame. A corollary of this is that no matter how much time we assign, most students will wait to motivate until the deadline looms. This seems natural and even sensible when they have so many things to juggle day in and day out. Therefore assigning eight weeks for a project and thinking students will spend eight weeks on it does not make a lot of sense. Students can often get done what they need to in several intensive sessions, so expect that and keep assigned time frames shorter, with the emphasis on doing it, rather than waiting to do it. Remember, however, that the strongest and most serious students will take much longer to produce a quality project. Time frames should not be so tight that they actually discourage quality creation.

When designing projects it is important to remember we value what we measure. As I want to promote student creativity and imaginative responses to the task, I denote these criteria as essential on the assessment rubric and award significant points for them. What I am generally looking for is a balance of technical skill, organization and focus, adherence to the task, creativity, and a uniquely imaginative response. On different projects we may emphasize different criteria, depending on how students have responded to previous project work. For example, if time management is no longer a problem for students in this particular group, we would decrease its value on the rubric.

To summarize, among the criteria for successful major projects are:

- emphasis on quality presentation
- emphasis on organization and task focus
- emphasis on time management in an extended though specific time frame
- room for individual student interpretation of task components
- encouragement of student creativity and imagination
- provision for some student self-assessment
- multidisciplinary, integrative approaches within a single project
- opportunities for students to demonstrate skills beyond what we ask for in written tests
- opportunities for less verbal and/or more artistic students to express their learning in new ways
- meaningful homework tasks around the project creation
- linking course curricula with multimedia exploration
- providing models of prior exemplary projects

PROJECT ASSESSMENT RUBRIC

Once student project work becomes a normal, ongoing aspect of the coursework, many advantages are realized. More students will participate in the life of the classroom and feel that they have a legitimate place. Students will make stronger learning connections as they integrate work in a range of disciplines, including language arts, visual arts, research, computer technology, and social studies. Students will look forward to the creative opportunities available to them through project work that is alternative to the regular "text and test" grind. The classroom itself becomes something of a museum or art gallery with quality student work displayed in abundance and with exhibits growing and changing with the creation of new projects.

ANTIGONE STORYBOARD	4	3	2	1
	EXCELLENT	QUALITY	ACCEPTABLE	NOT ACCEPTABLE
Name _____ CRITERIA				
Met general expectations 1. Name on bottom of art 2. Appropriate use of materials and equipment 3. As assigned 4. Completed on time	—	—	—	—
Demonstrated knowledge of play 1. Portrayed characters realistically 2. Described important elements 3. Captured essential theme	—	—	—	—
Used principles of art that apply 1. Balance 2. Variety (contrast) 3. Repetition (rhythm)	—	—	—	—
Showed creativity and effort 1. Expressed feeling, mood, and/or idea 2. Original and imaginative 3. Showed individuality, own style, point of view 4. Pleasing to look at or evoked intended response	—	—	—	—
Showed skill and craftsmanship 1. Developed control of materials 2. Developed control of techniques 3. Developed control of elements of art 4. Developed control of principles of art	—	—	—	—

Grading:

20 = 100	14 = 88	9 = 78
19 = 98	13 = 86	8 = 76
18 = 96	12 = 84	7 or below = Redo
17 = 94	11 = 82	
16 = 92	10 = 80	
15 = 90		

Thoughtful and extensive project work holding to a quality emphasis breathes life into the daily curriculum. Students achieve in new ways while expanding their conception of their own abilities. Among the many advantages to major project work are:

- increased interest in coursework through varied assessments
- increased opportunities for students to demonstrate learning and abilities
- heightened learning through integrative connections
- enhanced student ownership of classroom experience through project presentation and display
- continuity and meaning in homework over an extended time frame
- aesthetic improvement and visual interest in classroom through project display
- increased student control over the assessment process and resultant opportunities for higher achievement

When it comes to weighting major projects, a teacher has to determine how much is involved on the student's part. I generally equate a major project with a test or lengthy, out-of-class, written assignment. One need not be overly fine in the distinctions here, as it is counterproductive to split assessment atoms. Students need to know up front that a major project will result in a major grade, and we can leave it at that.

At the end of a quarter in my honors English section we might have three to five minor assignments I have evaluated; three to five I have not evaluated, only checked; one or two major papers; one or two major projects; one or two public speaking presentations; and perhaps one test. In my remedial English classes we would have about half as many major assignments and several spelling and grammar quizzes that I would not give to the honors students, who spell and write quite well already.

In a different subject with different student needs and capabilities, this formula would vary. What matters is to provide students with a range of teaching/learning experiences also assessed in a variety of ways. This range should include shorter and longer, more simple and more complex assignments and challenges. Major projects provide students with fresh and elaborate ways of expressing knowledge. The more time we provide for such expression, the richer the curriculum becomes.

Homework

AHH, HOMEWORK

Homework is often a large factor in a student's grade. Homework is also a powerful stressor in the lives of many children and their families. And the proper assigning, managing, and assessing of homework is problematic for many teachers as well.

I will be candid on this point, risking eternal ostracism from the traditionalist teaching pantheon: Most typical teacher-assigned homework is terribly overrated as a means of accomplishing anything much. In fact, speaking as a lifelong educator and longtime parent of honor roll students, I must say that most homework proves more detrimental than helpful to achievement of our avowed goals of furthering learning and interest in learning. In a word, it is all too often counterproductive. In the lives of many children, homework often competes with perfectly acceptable alternative activities, many of which have sound educational or personal value. That is added reason for careful application of the homework salve.

Keep this in mind, if nothing else, regarding homework: *The cumulative grade received from homework should never be the determining factor in a student's passing a class, whether for the quarter, semester, or year.*

CHILDHOOD'S END?

In an era when childhood is increasingly institutionalized, controlled more and more closely by adult-supervised activities, and/or manipulated by electronic media experiences, we need to be certain we are guarding our children's childhood, at least as much as we are preparing them to be productive employees and reliable consumers. If given a choice, I would rather see elementary children outside playing on autumn afternoons than sitting before video monitors or with their noses buried in textbooks—just playing those completely unproductive games that stimulate imagination and cultivate a range of wonderfully less measurable intelligence than homework ever could. I would rather see middle school children playing sports and games and finding time for plays and music groups. I would rather see high school children so engaged, as well, without having two or three hours of homework awaiting them after a late, rushed supper.

A recent study by the University of Michigan found that grade school students on average spent more than two hours a night on homework during the school year, up from 85 minutes in 1981. "I worry that too much homework kills that intrinsic desire to learn and explore," says Katherine Schultz, assistant professor of education at Penn State University, quoted in the *New York Times* (Newman 2000). "It's not going to make it more likely for them to get into Yale or Harvard when they get more homework."

Ten year-old Garret Mitchell of Montclair, New Jersey, says, "I like school ten times more than I like homework, but that's life." A gritty lesson for a child to swallow night after tedious night.

As we rush headlong into the standards-raising miasma, children all over the country are not only getting more homework, but receiving more involved summer projects as well (Newman 2000). In our school, my colleague Peter and I are pressured by the principal to give an extensive summer reading and writing project to the entering tenth-grade honors students. Our feeling is that they do plenty during the school year, and plenty during the summer, and that summer assignments are for the most part "we-are-academically-rigorous" CYA politics for the parents' benefit. Of course no one has actually polled the parents, many of whom doubtless would agree with Peter and me and leave the kids unhassled by school for a couple of months.

Ahh, but you say that summer world of catching bugs and riding bikes is gone. Kids will only be watching TV or surfing the net if they are not properly occupied with homework year-round. That is not my experience.

For the most part the kids who do the most homework are also the kids who have the most extracurricular interests and opportunities. Giving extra homework to all kids because we think it might gainfully occupy some kids makes little sense. This is especially so at the early elementary level where there are no data to suggest that homework enhances learning (U.S. Department of Education 1997). Setting up individual learning contracts with kids who can use extra time and encouragement, however, is sensible and can prove beneficial.

School days are getting longer, and school years are getting longer. Millions of low achieving inner-city students now go to what amounts to nearly year-round school. Seven to eight hours of school per day is a lot, not to mention early dropoffs and afterschool programs. Can't we get most of the learning accomplished in that substantial amount of time? If not, what are we doing for seven to eight hours a day? That might be a better question than how much more homework and summer projects we ought to load on the little buggers. School schedules and curricular priorities are for another book, however (please see Raebeck 1998).

It might be interesting for the reader to know that in Japanese schools, often heralded by Americans for their rigor and focus, students receive *far less* instruction in mathematics, and *far less* homework in mathematics, while often outperforming U.S. students on standardized exams in math (Newman 2000). Hmmm.

Again I implore us to remember what it was like to be a child. And that glorious, magical time passes so quickly. What is the rush, after all? I will always remember a summer day when our youngest daughter was about six, and our middle girl was ten. We were trying to organize some new activity for them, somehow anxious that their summer would not lead directly to an increase in the gross national product. Tessa looked up from her dolls and said imploringly, "We jus wanna pway!"

We succumbed to their desire to *just play* and have studiously attempted to maintain a healthy balance between their structured and unstructured experiences ever since, with a great degree of success, I might add. All three of our girls are productive, successful, and yet able to relax and enjoy the many delightful parts of life beyond the gradebook or the balance sheet.

HOMEWORK THAT HELPS

Now that I have your attention, we need to share a few additional observations. First of all, there is homework, and then there is homework. Homework that fits sound educational criteria can make sense and enhance our goals.

Homework that has several or all of the following elements can work just fine. It ought to:

- engage the student
- lead to new interests and observations
- provide for student direction
- reinforce important class learning
- be clear and doable
- be accomplishable in a reasonable time frame
- be fairly and appropriately assessed
- not count overmuch in the grading scheme

Does your experience with homework, either as a teacher, parent, or both, fit these criteria? Reading a book, especially a student-selected book, is an exemplary homework assignment. Doing a series of math problems to practice from the day's lesson is fine, too, so long as they are few in number, not numbingly repetitious. Working on a project at home is often more practical for many students and their teachers than working on it at school and fits our criteria. Reviewing one's notes in a quiet setting with study guidelines can be useful. Writing short or long papers, doing research, and memorizing lines for a skit are all valuable uses of out-of-class time.

This is not the case for all students, however.

LIMITATIONS OF HOMEWORK FOR
LESS ADVANTAGED STUDENTS

In chapter 1, I spoke to the demographics of a two-tiered grading pattern in school mirroring that of economic society beyond the school. One-third of our adult population has no more than a high school diploma, and but one-fourth holds a four-year college diploma. We also know that fully one-fifth of all children in the United States lives in poverty, with millions more just above that line and not a whole lot better off. This combination of low educational achievement and low income provides marginal conditions for learning in most cases.

It is a dangerously false assumption to think that each school child is sitting at home in a private, well-furnished bedroom, with a new computer, brimming bookshelves, TV restrictions, hearty meals, a pleasant sibling or two, regular bedtimes, and two parents on call for assistance and encouragement. It is far more likely that anything that many a low-income child accomplishes at home is done not because of the local environment but in spite of it.

This is a gentle reminder to us that many Americans are not living anything close to a "dream." Though teachers are of course generally aware of what our students have to contend with, we sometimes forget that their lives are markedly different from our own. Contending with a household situation that is far from ideal makes the seemingly simple act of doing homework a greater chore than we can imagine for some of these children. Rather than beating kids up over their failure to produce at home, we need to understand causes and seek solutions rather than impose additional penalties on top of their severe day-to-day struggles.

With that in mind I have found that with low-income, low-achieving kids the more I can do for and with them in school, where I can control the learning conditions to greater degree, the higher the rate of success. The less I expect them to accomplish outside of the school environment, the more reasonable my expectations. This sounds like a double standard, and risks creating a self-fulfilling prophecy. On the other hand we all know that understanding the learning styles and living conditions of children is crucial in developing potentially successful approaches.

This past year in my remedial English 12 classroom I had an interesting group of young adults. I will describe them below (changing their names of course), and you see if your remedial rosters are all that different from mine.

Tommy Chung: twenty-year-old Chinese immigrant struggling with English, parents still in China, working from 3 P.M. until after midnight delivering for relatives' Chinese restaurant seven days a week. Wonderfully nice young man, bright and conscientious. Also totally exhausted, barely able to keep his eyes open at 8 A.M. in our first period class. Drops out mid-year when he realizes he won't graduate anyway. Moves to northern Virginia to work in another Chinese restaurant with his brother.

Eva Grolsky: eighteen-year-old Polish immigrant, came to United States with her parents three years previous, but they have since returned to Poland. Lives on her own in small apartment, wears loads of eye make-up and MTV clothes, works every day in delicatessan, wants to be a model. Poses as a tough cookie but is crying inside. Although bilingual and highly intelligent, drops out in last quarter when she realizes she cannot pass a science course needed for graduation. Says she will return to Poland when she saves enough for ticket.

Ray Bonzee: nineteen-year-old Native American boy, living on a local reservation. Severe learning and attention issues. Never ruled eligible for special services until we (staff and his caring mother) insisted on yet another evaluation as a first semester senior. He finally qualifies as ADD and LD. Bright, at times quite charming, young man who takes native heritage seriously, traveling around the country to pow-wows. Has drinking problem and is constantly in trouble in school, largely due to boredom with his remedial classes, as well as anger and attention issues. Was an A student in fifth grade, all downhill since. Barely graduates and has no future plans.

Alejandro Correrra: nineteen-year-old Mexican immigrant. Handsome and talented as an artist. Loves soccer and is quite capable but after stellar sophomore year does not participate his junior year because coach would not allow him to play after he missed/didn't know about summer practices due to working with his father as a landscaper. Ineligible because of age as a senior. Well-spoken in English, he also reads the language better than many native English speakers after just five years here. Cannot accept that American colleges would want a student like him, even though his guidance counselor and I repeatedly tell him that he can go to any number of colleges and receive scholarship assistance for art, soccer, or both. Future plans uncertain.

Candace Smith: Apparently hostile girl, age eighteen. Has giant chip on her shoulder but is actually quite sweet at times. Has lost her father (to whom she was extremely close) the previous year to cancer. Thought to be of low average intelligence, Candi produces many excellent pieces of work in class, including a poem later published in the literary magazine. In constant warfare with her mother, she is a young adult who wants so much to be out of high school but has no thought of how she is going to survive. Smokes and parties as much as possible.

Dorita Santezzarro: Another immigrant, this time from Colombia, nineteen years old. An absolutely beautiful, stylish young woman, sensitive and refined. She reads and speaks English far better than one might expect as she has only been in this country two years. Like Eva and Tommy, her parents are not with her, and she has her own place, working daily after school to pay for that and her car. She is late to school most days and misses two or three days a week for much of the year. But in the final quarter she begins coming to class almost every day, producing quality work on a routine basis, as well. She talks of community college next year. We hope so.

Joey Jones: Eighteen years old, a lively, street-smart, hip-hop loving African American kid, athletic and a chronic underachiever. Does not read well and writes no better, hating English, mainly as a result of not being able to do it. Raised by his grandfather, it is his grandmother, an articulate and concerned college professor in the city, who cares most for Joey and attempts to monitor his activities from afar. He is a bit of a lost soul, somewhat annoying yet still a lovable kid looking at a difficult transition into the adult world. Says he wants to be a stand-up comedian. He has never qualified for special services, as his below average IQ is not discrepant enough with his reading ability. The system therefore provides him with no additional formal support, though he is desperate for just that. Joey talks about going to a state college, mainly because "going to college" is what high school seniors feel compelled to talk about. He is going nowhere so far as anyone can tell. However, you never know.

These are just some of my students in a single class in a normal year. Real kids with all too real challenges and problems. Try as they might, even as seniors, they cannot control so many of the aspects of academic and socioeconomic success in their lives. They are working to survive in several cases, and in others their lifelong track record of school frustration and failure makes further effort on their part almost foolish. Some of them have neither homes nor developed academic abilities. What can we reasonably expect of them outside of school, when simply enabling them to be relatively productive in school is a major victory? How many battles do we need to fight here?

Getting deeply ensnared in the "You-didn't-do-your-homework-and-now-you-must-pay" trap is a dead-end street with too many students struggling simply to get to bed before midnight and then to get up again before seven. We ought to understand the conditions of success and the realistic constraints.

I still assign some homework to my remedial students but not anything close to what the honors kids get. And my consequences for "lates" and "not dones" in this area are often less severe with these kids. It is not because I care less about these kids or believe one iota less in their potential. Just the contrary. I ask less of them outside my classroom because I can accept that asking too much is simply creating a no-win situation for them. They can win, and some of them will win eventually. But their victory is more likely when we adjust the rules a bit in their favor every now and then. This is not pampering or pandering—it is simply removing arbitrary and ultimately unnecessary obstacles for kids who already have a basketful too many.

TO GIVE AND NOT TO GIVE: HOW MUCH HOMEWORK?

Once we decide on the type of homework and its appropriateness for the group we are dealing with, the next decision relates to how much. There are written homework guidelines for various grades in many school districts. It generally has to do with common sense, based on a shared philosophy of education. If homework is to be effective, following the criteria defined earlier, then it has to be the right amount for the student. Let's think about what a typical child's life is like, the benefits of appropriate homework, the importance of nonschool activities, and the time available after school, and we can determine a sensible approach.

When I see teachers assigning homework on holiday vacations it makes me wonder what world they live in. What is a vacation, for goodness sake? Do we really think that students will fall apart after three to five days without school or that there is little else of import in their lives and we must continually provide meaning? Giving kids homework on weekends and vacations makes school, and teachers, more tedious and unlikable. Again we forget what it was like to be a student.

I *do* give students (a) short written or reading homework on any school night, Monday through Thursday, (b) papers or projects over longer periods of time, one–two weeks generally, when the students can determine their own approach and time frame, and (c) extensive reading assignments over several weeks, with recommended reading rates per day to keep up with the book.

I *do not* (a) give students written homework assignments on weekends or vacations, or (b) surprise them with extensive assignments due in a day or two.

STAYING IN TOUCH

As with other aspects of my teaching relationship with students, I attempt to remain open and listen to them when they have things to tell me. Contrary to national myth, students in honors and advanced placement courses have large workloads, lots of homework, and near constant exams. When they plead with me as a group that things are piling up, other assignments are due, or they have three major tests on the same day that I wish to assign something, I try to respond.

My goal is not to teach them that the world is a cold and demanding place where one either kills or is killed, either gets an Ivy League degree or vacuums sewer grates. My goal is to assist and encourage them to become better English students through developing important skills and increasing their appreciation, even love, of the beauty and power of our language. In my experience this goal is accomplished best through forging alliances with students and establishing standards of fairness and support, as well as rigor and quality.

The same attitude is in place when they tell me that the time frame for a major project or reading of a novel is too tight. We will re-examine it, look at our options. It is possible that I was overly ambitious when I laid it out or that I forgot we would lose an extra day to some event or trip or unexpected interference. I listen to their view. Sometimes they are wrong, a few slackers are just scraping for time, and they probably won't do it on time even when given the extension. Or perhaps they think the reading will take longer, until I show them the print size, or break it down to X pages per day. The point is that these issues are open to discussion in our classroom.

And if their request makes sense I will modify the time frame accordingly. All this in the name of classroom rapport, of keeping our eyes on the prize of reaching loftier goals than simply pushing through things to get them finished by often arbitrary deadlines.

ASSESSING HOMEWORK APPROPRIATELY

As minor nightly homework assignments are a minor part of the program they are graded accordingly. Checks are most often employed. Sometimes I assign marks of 1, 2, 3 to them. If it is a major project or paper done over many nights, then the standards of grading such are used.

What is key here is to keep homework in its proper place, and not assign so much weight to a single small piece of it that a low score, or failure to complete, will influence the student's grade unduly. Never give a zero for an incomplete or undone homework assignment (see "No Zeros" in chapter 2).

When we assign homework we want students to know that we believe it is worth doing, that we will look at it, and that we will hold students accountable for its completion. With those factors in mind, the assignment of nightly homework during the school week assumes its place as a relatively small, though still meaningful, part of the teaching/learning web for both older and younger students. Larger, more involved projects remain an essential and central part of that web, though primarily for our older students.

If homework is a hassle in your class, revisit your attitude and approach toward the giving and receiving of it. And remember, kids are kids. They often grow up pretty well despite our best efforts. We are not preparing them for battle with Martian invaders. There is no need to burn them out totally on education by the time they hit puberty or finish them off shortly thereafter. They can always squeeze into corporate cubicles later if they are unable to find anything more creative or compelling.

5

Cultivating Student Ownership
of the Grading Process

Teachers strive to develop students' sense of quality and their sense of the effort required for producing works of quality. Directly involving students in the assessment process is central to our effort. The more that students understand the grading process, see its potential benefit, and participate in its development, the more power they have and the more they care about their outcomes. Human history confirms that people are most productive over time when they have ownership in the process and the process itself is meaningful. This is one reason democratic capitalism tends to be more successful than communism or other despotic socioeconomic models (Landes 1999).

When we tightly control the means of assessment and also conceal its formulas, we frustrate, alienate, and sometimes even anger students. This promotes feelings of powerlessness and forced conformity where we claim to desire intelligence, free thinking, and open questioning. This is a fancy way of saying students (and teachers) benefit when students understand and participate in the assessment and grading process. William Glasser's somewhat revolutionary control theory is all about the personal and social gains inherent in people having control over their own actions and productivity (Glasser 1985; Glasser 1990). The teacher functions more as a coach, mentor, arbiter, facilitator, and leader rather than merely an enforcer, ruler, and controller. The teacher's role remains a strong, central one. For control theory (with its emphasis on "the three Rs" of reality, responsibility, and

right and wrong) demands individual accountability wile fostering psychological health.

CLEAR CRITERIA OPENLY SHARED

Students ought to always know exactly how they are being assessed and
precisely what criteria they are being graded on. If the teacher knows the
criteria, then they must be thoroughly explained. If the teacher is unsure,
then the assessment process must be modified until the teacher is sure.
Then it can be properly shared with students.

With every major assignment, I share everything about the assessment criteria up front. I give the students a copy of the same rubric I will use to determine their grade. Over time the focuses and criteria are modified as it becomes apparent that one element or another is less important and additional
elements need be considered. We must constantly remember that teacher-
made instruments are subjective and by definition imprecise. Therefore crafting and recrafting rubrics with changing criteria to ensure optimal effectiveness is that much more important.

STUDENT–TEACHER DIALOGUE

The students are the guinea pigs in one sense, but guinea pigs who can
reason and speak. Good teachers listen to their students and regularly so-
licit feedback. Maintaining constructive dialogue with our students provides teachers with excellent, up-to-date information regarding the impact
of our assessment instruments and strategies. What is more, it greatly increases student ownership of the teaching/learning process.

Dialogue may occur around several aspects of assessment, including
what, when, how, and why. Students may tell us that one element of the
rubric is weighted too much, another too little. They may ask that more
emphasis go to creativity with a certain project and less to organization or
vice versa. Or they may tell us that something is not clear, that they do not
understand what is meant by "an engaging introduction," for example.
Our thoughtful responses to their queries will only aid their success.

Research Report Rubric

Student's Name ⎯⎯⎯⎯⎯⎯⎯⎯⎯⎯⎯⎯

Grade ⎯⎯⎯⎯⎯

	Self		Teacher (Excellent)	(Capable)	(Partial)	(Minimal)
	Yes	No	4	3	2	1
Title Page: ⇒						
Capitalized and spelled correctly						
Lower right hand corner—name and date						
Table of Contents:						
Capitalized and spelled correctly						
Page numbers listed						
Report: Contents (×2) ⇒						
Introduction grabs the attention of the reader						
Is easily understood/clear expression						
Sticks to the main topic or theme						
Includes author's own ideas and words						
Has balance of factual information and human perspectives (emotions and feelings)						
Arranged in sequential order						
Report: Mechanics ⇒						
4–6 pages typed						
Correct margins used						
Correct paragraphing						
Correct spelling (fewer than 3 errors)						
Correct grammar and punctuation						
Proper endnotes						
Illustrations: ⇒						
Two illustrations are included in report						
Illustrations are labeled						
Illustrations are relevant to topic or theme						
Illustrations appear neat and organized						
Bibliography: ⇒						
Five sources are listed						
Correct bibliography form is used						
Draft (×2) ⇒						

Grading:

32 = 100	28 = 92	24 = 84	20 or below =
31 = 98	27 = 90	23 = 82	Redo
30 = 96	26 = 88	22 = 80	
29 = 94	25 = 86	21 = 78	

When we actually incorporate their thinking into a revised assessment instrument they clearly see that their involvement is valued.

Recently my tenth-grade daughter spent an amazing amount of time and effort on a research paper about Osama bin Laden and his international terrorist network. I watched her work for weeks on the project and turn out an exceptional product. She is a strong honors English student, and her goal was to produce a perfect paper. She understood the criteria and received excellent feedback on her draft, with but one teacher suggestion, that being that she modify the way she was reporting an element of the bibliography. She did exactly what *she thought* the teacher had requested, making the changes she thought he wanted.

Yet she was quite disappointed when she received her final grade, because two points were taken off for the bibliography. You see, she had made the change but had either misunderstood the teacher's direction or perhaps he had not been clear enough in explaining what he wanted. She had not made the same mistake twice. All she did was try to comply, yet she got penalized for it. I suggested she speak with the teacher to explain, but she was rebuffed when she did so. To me that is not fair. I would give the student the benefit of the doubt in that situation—especially one as conscientious as Emily was in this case. A teaching opportunity was lost, and a good student frustrated and discouraged as a result.

STUDENT SELF-ASSESSMENT

Another way to develop student ownership of the grading experience is to incorporate student self-assessment into it. In my classes students are sometimes asked to hand in a self-assessment rubric with most major projects and papers. I do not include this in the grade, but I do want the students to personalize their understanding of the criteria as much as possible. Doing a self-assessment assists in this matter. When our results differ significantly we have grounds for discussion and deeper understanding. Sometimes I am compelled to change my assessment when a student shares his or her unique perspective with me, perhaps pointing out something that I failed to take into account or missed entirely.

When students do such public performances as readings, skits, or teaching lessons, we often set up two or three students as a panel of peer assessors. They use the same rubric I do and provide their copies to me as the student presenters complete their performances. Generally we are quite close in our assessments. When we differ substantially, and there is consensus among the peer panel, I will take that into consideration and factor the panel's findings into my final grading.

PROMPT, EVEN IMMEDIATE, FEEDBACK

There is sound evidence indicating that feedback is more effective the closer it is to the event, performance, paper, or test, and that its impact declines in direct correlation to the interval of time between the event and the feedback (Jensen 1998). With this in mind I always try to provide feedback as quickly as possible. With the many classroom performances my students do individually, in pairs, and in small groups, they receive instantaneous feedback.

I have the rubrics in front of me, and I make the proper notations while the performance (recitation, skit, public speech, poetry reading) is going on. At its completion I quickly compute the rubric areas and convert the numbers to a grade, based on the attached scale. This is a bit hectic for me, and I have to work hard to be accurate with all the hubbub of one group finishing, another one preparing, and the class instantly falling into social conversations (or something potentially much worse, like high stakes poker games or spin the bottle).

But usually I am able to compute the grades and provide them to the students while they're on their way back to their seats. They appreciate the instant feedback, and I am not left with a lot of forms to grade later. Although a bit harrying, this provision of instant feedback serves us well.

I do the same thing with quizzes, almost always grading them as they are handed in, with the students standing there awaiting the results. It increases interest, prevents paper buildup for me, and provides the immediate feedback students desire and respond to.

CLASSROOM PARTICIPATION GRADE

Strong teachers use many factors in determining grades. We do not simply crunch numbers. The human factor is taken into account. We want to acknowledge those who are our good citizens and hard workers. We want to stimulate those who are working at less than capacity or subverting the social dynamic in some way. Yet most secondary schools do not give formal grades for behavior or effort or citizenship.

These are important components of success, however. And no matter what we would like to believe about ourselves, we cannot separate a student's attitude from his or her performance. Nor should we.

Rather than ignore this issue, I intentionally compute it into a student's grade. I do this by providing students with a classroom participation grade each quarter. It is the equivalent of a major grade and is averaged in as such with the other grades. As with other assessments, the criteria are shared with students (and parents) at the beginning of the school year. I want them to know that these factors of daily performance, beyond tests, quizzes, homework, and major projects, will significantly influence their grade. At the same time, this approach enables me to emphasize eleven positive aspects of classroom behavior. This clarifies and reinforces what we value in the classroom gestalt.

When I share these forms with students I put a check next to the areas of growth and strength and a minus next to the areas where improvement is required. This sparks student response, especially when an item is minused but the student thinks that it shouldn't have been or when an item is not checked and the student thinks that it should have been. As with other areas of assessment, I try to listen to students' concerns, and I am perfectly willing to revise the form if a student is convincing enough.

More often than not the form stays as I checked it, with the understanding that the student has control over future marks, based on performance. "You don't agree? Do something about it by next time." This can be a stimulus for renewed effort as well.

I share the class participation grades at mid-quarter in the first marking period, as an interim behavior grade (our school already asks us to provide an interim academic grade). And I tell students that the grade can go up or down in the ensuing weeks, depending on their attention to these

Classroom Participation Grade

Dr. Raebeck

Factors:

Thoughtfulness of Comments

Willingness to Comment, Share, and Present

Cooperation

Respect for Others and Their Views

Speaking in Turn

Attentiveness

Positive Attitude

Responsiveness to Teacher

Responsiveness to Classmates

Attendance

Punctuality

Student: _____   Grade: _____

factors. Quite often this process provokes students to recommit, and their class participation grades rise accordingly by the end of the quarter.

What seems to work here is that specific behavioral criteria are detailed and students are receiving precise feedback on elements of classroom participation and behavior that are often ignored or assessed in a less accurate or precise way. They feel that they can control the outcomes to a great degree. And this promotional cataloging of positive behavior serves as an impctus to development of just such behavior, quite often even with the most challenging students.

LISTENING TO STUDENTS' REASONS, EXCUSES, AND NONSENSE

Modern life is complicated. When I begin an academic year I know that during the next ten months my students en toto will travail the full range of human experience. For along with the daily pleasures, successes, and even the occasional triumph, they will have sickness, injury, accidents, the loss of a special pet, broken friendships and relationships, mental depression, economic hardship, relocation, and even divorce, violence, or the death of a friend, sibling, grandparent, or parent. No one gets through this world unscathed, and calamity can strike at any moment.

These young people have hectic and at times traumatic lives. Not every day goes well. Sometimes Dr. Raebeck's homework cannot be the priority. When students come to me with excuses for not getting something done, whether it is last night's reading or a major term paper, I listen to them before assigning penalties. What I need to determine is the why. If they share reasonable explanations, who am I to doubt and punish them? As I get to know my students I can generally tell, as experienced teachers can, when they are sincere and when they are slacking. But initially there is no pattern, so I always try at first to respect their reasons rather than condemn those as excuses.

"Hey," I'll ask them, "can you get it in tomorrow? How much time do you need?" They are delighted with the second chance and relieved to not have to tell me too much sometimes because the reasons can be embarrassing, especially when they are due to family circumstances beyond the student's control. I don't pry, knowing that it may not be my business. What I want to do is encourage and support, at first. I am not particularly worried about being taken advantage of.

Not so long ago in my honors class a clearly upset student came to me with her problem. She had turned in a major theme paper, and it was so fraught with mistakes that I had stopped correcting it after one paragraph and asked her to rewrite and resubmit it. As it turned out, this young woman had just been through an ugly incident with her boyfriend and criminal proceedings were under way. The boy and a friend of his were continuing to harass her, and she was an emotional mess. She had commenced the writing of the paper at the apex of this dilemma, clearly unable to concentrate. Yet at the same time, she was committed to doing well in the course and felt this situation currently ruining her life outside of the classroom was now negatively impacting it inside the classroom. She needed more time, another chance.

I already knew of her situation from informed colleagues, and it was easy for me to grant her additional time, without penalty, to complete the writing. Most teachers would do the same thing in that circumstance. But it is not always that obvious, and students will share and protect personal information in different ways. It is up to us to anticipate that and to accept the reality that at any given time some of our students are suffering, and even in crisis. We need to be there for them at just those times.

When the student fails to deliver on the second chance or consistently shirks assignments or ignores deadlines, we likely have a different type of issue, and consequences may be in order. At the beginning, however, we are trying to establish trust and respect, along with sound habits. Giving people another chance is often an excellent way to promote productivity in the long run. We are trying to teach many things, not just promptness and responsibility, important as those are. One rarely loses by being generous.

When a student knows that I have listened, knows that I recognize the value of his or her situation, that student is just as likely to feel more responsibility next time than to take advantage. Experience has borne this: For every student who abuses my understanding and flexibility, there are several who appreciate and never abuse that. That was certainly the case with the girl who needed another crack at her theme paper. The one she ultimately handed in was representative of her ability and something she could be proud of. As a result, her academic year got off to a much better start. She did quite well from that point forward.

STUDENTS TEACHING

Along with involving students in the discussion of grading philosophy and being flexible with their needs and interests, we can also involve them directly in the teaching process. By having our students teach at times, we

- advance their sense of ownership
- provide variety and stimulus for the group
- give ourselves a break and a different role for a time
- enhance student learning

After all, teaching something is an excellent way to learn it. (See "Chapter Masters," chapter 8.) Including students in the actul teaching process is another way to build a sense of ownership and shared purpose. This develops a feeling that "we are all in this together." And that feeling is a good one.

6

Rubrics

The use of rubrics has been referred to briefly several times previously in this book. Here I will discuss their efficacy in greater detail. I have been using rubrics with high school and college students for many years. At this point I can say with assurance that rubrics greatly enhance the teaching/learning experience, while making assessment criteria and related grades clear and fair. In fact, since I provide rubrics for every major project and assignment, I am currently known in some professional circles as Dr. Rubric. I like that. I like rubrics. They work.

THE RUBRIC ITSELF

Rubrics are printed grids that show both the criteria to be assessed and the various levels of assessment possible. Each assessment level is equated with a number score, such as 4, 3, 2, 1. The scores are tallied in a simple addition process. On my rubrics (see table 8.2) I include the translation of the rubric total score into a number grade (more on this in "Rubrics, Grades, and Weighting" later in this chapter).

Most of us are now at least somewhat familiar with rubrics. They are easy to make, with the availability of prearranged tables and charts on any word processing software. Once a template is created, modification of it or creation of a new one for another assignment takes just minutes.

ESTABLISHING CRITERIA: LESS IS MORE

A strong feature of rubrics is that they clarify the assessment criteria up front. This demystifies grading and enables students to understand what the rules of the game are. At the same time, because pre-established criteria set up a framework, that same framework can be easily modified over time as the assignments change in terms of scope and accessibility.

Defining and redefining criteria provide a reflective exercise for the teacher. I am able to clarify objectives, determine priorities and emphases, and rearrange aspects of an assignment in the ongoing attempt to make each project experience as valuable for students as possible. At the same time I have learned to resist the impulse to make things increasingly complex by layering in new elements without skimming off the old. No, I do not want clutter and confusion.

For me the simpler rubrics prove better. Those that are wordy and complex tend to be impenetrable for some students and teachers. The ones offered by New York State for grading the English Regents are examples of such. Sharing the elaborate and dense vocabulary of the descriptors in the six categories (two categories too many in my opinion) with students proves an exercise in futility. Somehow a typical eleventh-grade student will not muster nearly the excitement that a state department bureaucrat manages for such stuff. (See pp. 60–61.)

At the same time, an overly complex rubric forces the assessor to split hairs. There is much clearer delineation among the four areas of a four-point rubric than there is among the six areas of a six-point rubric. The same applies to the criteria areas. Too many areas with too much description can overlap or confuse the issue. The more elaborate the descriptors, the fewer the criteria is a rule of thumb here.

Good students will always receive the highest scores, no matter how the rubric is constructed. Too much information can be as limiting as too little. Time is tight and precious in schools. Simpler is generally better for the harried, overextended teacher. It is easier for the student, as well. Give it to me straight, dude.

RUBRICS, GRADES, AND WEIGHTING

Early proponents of rubrics saw them as a true alternative assessment and insisted that rubric numbers not be turned into grades (Wessels and Burkholz 1996). In the typical, grade-intensive atmosphere of most U.S. secondary schools, this seems overly idealistic, even impracticable. When I give major assignments, those require a major assessment, and so a grade is going to be attached most or all of the time. Tying grades to rubrics is actually quite simple and seems in no way counterproductive to establishing an ethic of quality work in the classroom. There is nothing educationally unsound about assigning a high grade to an excellent piece of student work or a low grade to a piece that leaves much to be desired from a student clearly capable of more (Marzano 2000).

Another advantage to creating rubrics and tying them directly to grades is the flexibility it provides the teacher in grading. First I decide how much a rubric point is worth in terms of a grade. If the rubric total possible is 32 points, that would translate to a 100 for a grade. But what is a 31? Do we simply divide the 32 into 100 and assign 3.12 grade points per rubric point? That's messy and cumbersome—too much arithmetic. So I approach this another way.

I think about what the points mean: 4, 3, 2, 1, 0. And I think about what getting mostly 4s ought to mean. Because if 4 means excellent, or exemplary, or outstanding, or "fullfilled fully," then getting mostly 4s ought to be a score in the 90s, or an A. If 3 means capable, or some such, then getting mostly 3s ought to be a score in the 80s, or a B. And so a rubric averaging in the 2s would be a C in my way of thinking. This all makes sense to my students, as I have never had a single one complain about the weighting of my rubrics. Again, my bias is to let students begin with a 100 rather than 0.

Determining which criteria to include in the rubric takes thought and experience, as does determining how to weight each criterion. If they are to be weighted equally, then one must be certain that one wants to equate *originality,* say, with *organization.* For the criteria we establish describes our teaching/learning priorities to our students. A simple way to build in a bit of

New York State English Regents

SESSION TWO—PART A—SCORING RUBRIC
READING AND WRITING FOR LITERARY RESPONSE

QUALITY	6 Responses at this level:	5 Responses at this level:	4 Responses at this level:	3 Responses at this level:	2 Responses at this level:	1 Responses at this level:
Meaning: the extent to which the response exhibits sound understanding, interpretation, and analysis of the task and text(s)	-establish a controlling idea that reveals an in-depth analysis of both texts -make insightful connections between the controlling idea and the ideas in each text	-establish a controlling idea that reveals a thorough understanding of both texts -make clear and explicit connections between the controlling idea and the ideas in each text	-establish a controlling idea that shows a basic understanding of both texts -make implicit connections between the controlling idea and the ideas in each text	-establish a controlling idea that shows a basic understanding of the texts -make few or superficial connections between the controlling idea and the ideas in the texts	-convey a confused or incomplete understanding of the texts -make a few connections but fail to establish a controlling idea	-provide minimal or no evidence of textual understanding -make no connections between the texts or among ideas in the texts
Development: the extent to which ideas are elaborated using specific and relevant evidence from the text(s)	-develop ideas clearly and fully, making effective use of a wide range of relevant and specific evidence and appropriate literary elements from both texts	-develop ideas clearly and consistently, with reference to relevant and specific evidence and appropriate literary elements from both texts	-develop some ideas more fully than others, with reference to specific and relevant evidence and appropriate literary elements from both texts	-develop ideas briefly, using some evidence from the texts -may rely primarily on plot summary	-are incomplete or largely undeveloped, hinting at ideas, but references to the text are vague, irrelevant, repetitive, or unjustified	-are minimal, with no evidence of development

Criterion						
Organization: the extent to which the response exhibits direction, shape, and coherence	-maintain the focus established by the controlling idea -exhibit a logical and coherent structure through skillful use of appropriate devices and transitions	-maintain the focus established by the controlling idea -exhibit a logical sequence of ideas through use of appropriate devices and transitions	-maintain a clear and appropriate focus -exhibit a logical sequence of ideas but may lack internal consistency	-establish, but fail to maintain, an appropriate focus -exhibit a rudimentary structure but may include some inconsistencies or irrelevancies	-lack an appropriate focus but suggest some organization, or suggest a focus but lack organization	-show no focus or organization
Language Use: the extent to which the response reveals an awareness of audience and purpose through effective use of words, sentence structure, and sentence variety	-are stylistically sophisticated, using language that is precise and engaging, with a notable sense of voice and awareness of audience and purpose -vary structure and length of sentences to enhance meaning	-use language that is fluent and original, with evident awareness of audience and purpose -vary structure and length of sentences to control rhythm and pacing	-use appropriate language, with some awareness of audience and purpose -occasionally make effective use of sentence structure or length	-rely on basic vocabulary, with little awareness of audience or purpose -exhibit some attempt to vary sentence structure or length for effect, but with uneven success	-use language that is imprecise or unsuitable for the audience or purpose -reveal little awareness of how to use sentences to achieve an effect	-are minimal -use language that is incoherent or inappropriate
Conventions: the extent to which the response exhibits conventional spelling, punctuation, paragraphing, capitalization, grammar, and usage	-demonstrate control of the conventions with essentially no errors, even with sophisticated language	-demonstrate control of the conventions, exhibiting occasional errors only when using sophisticated language	-demonstrate partial control, exhibiting occasional errors that do not hinder comprehension	-demonstrate emerging control, exhibiting occasional errors that hinder comprehension	-demonstrate a lack of control, exhibiting frequent errors that make comprehension difficult	-are minimal, making assessment of conventions unreliable -may be illegible or not recognizable as English

- If the student addresses only one text, the response can be scored no higher than a 3.
- If the student writes only a personal response and makes no reference to the text(s), the response can be scored no higher than a 1.
- Responses totally unrelated to the topic, illegible, incoherent, or blank should be given a 0.
- A response totally copied from the text(s) with no original student writing should be scored a 0.

Poetry Booklets

Student _____   Grade _____

	4	3	2	1
Quality of Ideas (meaning, importance of themes)				
Quality of Cover and General Design (appearance, design creativity, neatness)				
Descriptive Language (vocabulary, imagery, creativity)				
Using Eight Elements of Poetry Four Elements of Sound (meter, alliteration, repetition, rhyme)				
Four Elements of Meaning (metaphor, personification, simile, symbolism)				

Total _____

Scoring: 4 = Requirements *exceptionally* fulfilled
              3 = Requirements *capably* fulfilled
              2 = Requirements *partially* fulfilled
              1 = Requirements *minimally* fulfilled
              0 = Requirements *not* fulfilled

Grading:
20 = 100   16 = 88   12 = 76
19 = 97   15 = 85   Below 12 = Redo
18 = 94   14 = 82
17 = 91   13 = 79

success in a rubric is to give equal weight to a category that all students can easily fulfill, such as *length of paper* or *attention to task*. Sometimes I combine these categories into one so they do not have too much weight yet can still provide all but the least committed students with a baseline of a 4 in one area. In my rubrics now I "double-weight" mechanics of writing and "double-weight" content in a research paper.

At the same time, continuing the emphasis on productivity and success, we have an R on our rubrics here. The R stands for Redo. It is set somewhere in the C or 70s range, and a student who receives an R has to hand in a new paper or project or redo the task, skit, or performance. This establishes that high floor we spoke of early on. I do not accept unacceptable work. That is one major reason virtually no one fails in my classes.

This is actually the mastery learning approach and quite acceptable in terms of educational philosophy. We give a task to do that we feel is worthwhile. We expect it to be done well. If it is not, we insist that it be done over until it is brought to an acceptable level. At the same time, we will not allow full credit for a Redo, even if the work is exemplary the second time. For, as noted earlier, that would not be entirely fair to those who got it right the first time.

Assessments without Grades

Overgrading, a topic explored in chapter 2, is a practice to be avoided. Actually there are many classroom experiences that require no grades at all. Sometimes alternative assessments are appropriate, and sometimes little or no formal assessment is necessary to assist the teaching/learning process.

Experts on assessment believe that effective teacher assessment leads to effective student self-assessment (Marzano 2000; Wiggins 1993). Consequently students develop more sophisticated standards and produce higher quality work. One of my goals with students is to enable them to become increasingly reflective regarding their own work, relying less and less on my evaluations and more on their own perspective and developing standards. Formal teacher assessment can assist this process, but it can also retard it. So much of what we do in schools, as in life, requires no formal assessment at all. Below I will share several classroom practices requiring no formal assessment yet substantially enhancing the teaching/learning experience.

STUDENT WRITING: CORRECTING AND OVERCORRECTING

It is refreshing for students to have opportunities to write topically, or freely, but not have their writing critiqued. This is not to say that feedback from an accomplished, sensitive writer/teacher is not helpful. Of course it is. But it is not necessary continuously and can become counterproductive if offered too often or in too great detail. Overcorrecting, a form of overgrading, is a mistake English teachers routinely make when reading student work (Atwell 1987; Parsons 1990). Such overcorrecting will discourage, and may even paralyze, the less confident student. It seems sometimes as though veteran adult teachers feel a need to convince their far younger students how much they know as teachers. The goal is not to show off our own knowledge. What is more, so much of what we feel is definitely true about written expression is subject to interpretation and reinterpretation, as the language itself is under constant revision. That is the way a language behaves—it changes all the time. William Safire has made a career out of his weekly "On Language" column in the *New York Times Sunda*y magazine. (Should "magazine" be capitalized here? Would that assist our understanding? Does it matter at all?)

There remain many agreed upon points in language and learning, and certainly a central part of a teacher's responsibility is to at times show students a better way. The danger is in assuming the heavy mantle of authority and remaining draped in it no matter what the weather, what the situation. For teachers to state with final authority that a comma must be placed before "but" in a sentence, where a new paragraph ought to begin in a composition, or even whether to capitalize "Twentieth Century" is questionable at best. Usage, punctuation, and grammar all change dramatically over time, as language is plastic and trendy stuff. A fifteen-year-old version of *Warriner's English Grammar* may not be the best source for determining validity. We need remain humble. "The more I learn the less I know."

As a writer I can particularly identify with this problem of overcorrecting. Writing is a skill that improves with use, and much of that improvement can occur with little outside feedback. Some of the best ways to strengthen one's writing are to read, to write in a variety of modes, to write often and freely, to discuss with others one's writing instincts and purposes, to reread one's earlier work, and to use writing to respond to ideas or events in life or fiction.

RESPONSE JOURNALS

A good vehicle for students doing writing without correction is the response journal (see Parsons 1990). Periodically I will hand out the journals in class and ask students to respond to a prompt of some kind. Generally the prompt has to do with an idea in a book that we are reading, and it is as open-ended as possible. If we were midway through Dickens's *Great Expectations,* say, a prompt for a response might be:

> Please respond to the following: "At this point Pip is less clear about the benefits of his being an idle gentleman and even feels somewhat guilty about the decline of his friendship with Joe and Biddy. Have there been times when you got what you wanted but were less satisfied than you expected? Can you think of characters in books or films that had similar issues? Is it true that 'Money cannot buy happiness' or would you like to at least get rich before deciding?"

It is less important that students adhere to a precise response than it is that they simply get writing quickly and freely. If students wish to write about something indirectly related to the prompt, or even unrelated, that is usually acceptable. I want them to write and reflect, for writing is one of the best ways to teach thinking. Writing of the journal type is also an opportunity to be creatively expresssive, to write outside the lines. We ought to encourage our students to do this as much as possible, for so much of their academic endeavor is heavily circumscribed.

Although the journals can also serve as a freewriting exercise at times, using a response format to provide structure keeps us from wandering into the "any-writing-is-good-writing" desert. Along with the prompts, we remind students that their writing is important, that they are developing it as they go, and it ought to become clearer and stronger. Therefore, even though it will not be formally corrected, I will occasionally review the journals, and I remind the students that I expect that they will always follow the basic conventions of English. We never want to reinforce carelessness or build in bad habits with students old enough to know better.

LITERATURE CIRCLES

Just as students benefit from having more open-ended writing opportunities, they benefit from self-directed reading. After discovering Harvey Daniels's wonderful 1994 book *Literature Circles: Voice and Choice in the Student-Centered Classroom.* I began using his process in my classes.

The premise is that students need alternatives to the typical everyone-reads-the-same-novel-at-the-same-time reading experience. Literature circles form around several different books, plays, or stories, with students making decisions about what they wish to read. There is a definite structure here, however, with specific roles assigned within the student groups and those roles rotating regularly. The roles serve as the means for focusing the discussions that form around the readings. Students move through a book, a chapter, or a play, determining much of the pace and content themselves. We formed circles around several Shakespearean plays at once, with tenth-grade student groups working independently of one another, selecting and reading *Hamlet, Twelfth Night, Julius Caesar, As You Like It,* and *MacBeth,* among others.

Like any good process this one can be modified, and a single work may be approached through the literature circles method. I have done *Romeo and Juliet* in this manner, with student circles of four forming as the main means of discussing the play. I also may use some simple form of minor assessment to ensure a sustained focus, as I have sometimes found that with no accountability of this type some students in this setting for the first time will not produce at an expected level.

SOCRATIC SEMINARS

All too often classroom "discussion" is relegated to the familiar and pedestrian teacher-questions-and-students-answer mode. We all have learned about the importance of promoting higher order thinking by our students. Skilled teacher-led questioning can attain this end, when the teacher is reflective, sensitive, and able. It is far more likely, however, that even the capable teacher will unintentionally fall into the low-level ask-and-respond, hunt-and-peck kind of questioning that not only keeps the learning in the lower levels of Bloom's (1957) *Taxonomy of Educational Objectives* (primarily *recall* and *comprehension*) but also confines the experience to the more active or extroverted students. Usually discussions of this type are limited. Though they may seem interesting to the teacher, somewhat rewarding to the handful of student respondents comfortable with the format, and certainly can fill a typically short class time frame, they actually involve little genuine thinking of the types higher in the taxonomy (*analysis, synthesis* and *evaluation*) and rarely engage more than a small percentage of the students in the group.

Perhaps the best way I know of holding effective discussions in a class is the Socratic seminar. The experience derives its name from the techniques Socrates employed as described in the writings of Plato when Socrates as teacher offered an extensive series of questions designed to lead his pledges to a deeper comprehension of their own thought processes and values. What we obtain in a true Socratic seminar is widespread student participation, substantial higher order thinking, and consequently strong rates of student engagement. This formal exercise works wonderfully when the following tenets are adhered to.

1) Guiding questions of an open-ended and multifaceted type are established upfront, ideally provided to the students the day before the seminar. These shape the discussion.
2) Three roles are offered: facilitator, observer, participant (more on these roles following).
3) Participants are expected to behave maturely, wait their turn, and not to interrupt another speaker.
4) Participants can disagree with a position but not with a person, so they are taught to "agree to disagree agreeably."

The seminars work best with twelve to eighteen active participants and one facilitator. Two, three, or more students may serve as observers. (Obviously class size is a factor, but it should not be a sole deterrent. We can also extend the seminar an additional class period if we have a larger group and thus need more "air time.") The observers record who speaks and how often, how well the group adheres to the expected behaviors, how well the guiding questions are answered, and how capably the facilitator coordinates the process.

When we first do a seminar, I will serve as facilitator to demonstrate that role. The faciliator does not inject personal opinion nor critique anyone's responses. Rather, the facilitator keeps things moving by deciding when a question has sufficiently been dealt with, asks follow-up questions, draws out participants who have not yet spoken, and reminds the group of the rules, should that be necessary. After a couple of seminars I may ask a student to play the facilitator role. I sit next to the student facilitator and assist as little as possible, perhaps doing nothing more than whispering a suggestion to go on to the next question or to call on someone new. Choosing the facilitator is key, as you can see. When students are familiar with the seminar process and have successfully done several, I might even be a participant in one, making certain that I do not dominate.

What occurs in an effective seminar is remarkable. We get virtually full student participation, there is little or no interruption or argument, the observers (sitting outside the group and not allowed to participate) report afterwards that things have gone well, and most students emerge from the experience feeling that they have been part of a thoughtful and compelling discussion—assuming that they have, of course. The quality of the guiding questions, the interest level, and relevance to the students of the text, idea, or current event under discussion are crucial, as you might imagine.

No grades are given; the assessment is an informal group one provided verbally by the student observers at the close of the seminar. But teacher assessment does take place, of course. I learn a great deal about who is paying attention to the subject we're examining, and I also see previously hidden speaking and thinking abilities in students who are reticent to contribute in the more typical classroom teacher-controls/extroverts-are-rewarded scenario. Students quickly adapt to the Socratic formula, and seminars tend to be valuable throughout the year as a sound means of further exploring the curriculum.

PORTFOLIOS

Portfolios may be simple or elaborate, annual or cumulative, graded or not graded, and so forth. They can be used in a variety of ways or simply serve as a collection of student work. Keeping student work for extended periods of time and providing time in school for students to reflect on the value of that work and compare it to current work in terms of their own development is a valuable teaching/learning tool. Sharing it with parents/guardians at certain times is a valid means of further involving them in their children's academic endeavor. In our district we have been using portfolios for many years with somewhat varied results. They are easier to manage at the elementary and middle school level and less so at the high school level, where storage, maintenance, and review of these multidisciplinary portfolios fall to the English teachers.

English teachers at middle and high school levels everywhere often have writing portfolios that students build, and many elementary teachers generally catalog student work annually. What I like about the portfolio process is that it is a formal means for students to at least take some time periodically to note progress in various areas and to form additional pride in that progress.

There is no need for a grade in our system, though assessment is done in several ways. Students do much of the assessment themselves in determining how they have satisified certain district and state standards through the production of pieces of work in several disciplines. Our portfolios are large folders with categorized pockets wherein work is placed, selected for one of the various standards we deem most important.

Teachers assist in this assessment, speaking with students about their selection process, helping students choose among comparable work, and clarifying what is meant by those objectives less clear to the students. Teachers can recommend that a piece be placed here or there, but final determination is left to our students. This process of production, collection, reflection, and selection is an educationally valuable one. Although the individual pieces are usually graded by teachers, no grade is given in the portfolio process or to the accumulating portfolios themselves.

8

Grade-Friendly Projects:
Encouraging Student Success

PUBLIC SPEAKING

It is a truism that one of our deepest human anxieties has to do with standing up and talking formally in front of an audience. At the same time, should one become more or less comfortable in this arena, it is a powerful ability to possess. Believing this, I provide all of my students with opportunities to stand before the group and speak formally several times each year. As with virtually everything else we are afraid of in this world, once we do it, in most cases our fears abate. So speak publicly we do.

There are a few keys to success here. First we want to establish a fine balance of (a) support for students with (b) seriousness of purpose. We must be encouraging and not overly critical, especially with first efforts. At the same time we must have clear expectations and high standards for performance.

Second, it is appropriate, at least initially, to have short time frames. Asking novice speakers to prepare ten-minute talks will seem overwhelming. We also have the omnipresent time constraints that limit how many classes we wish to spend on any given task. Given normal classes of twenty to thirty students, a time frame of two to three minutes per speech is fine. With setup and feedback, it still may require up to ten minutes per student. Speeches much longer than this will necessarily mean two weeks of just these speeches. Naturally nervous students find it far more palatable to think in terms of two to three minutes rather than five to ten minutes for their early speaking efforts.

Selecting effective topics is our next concern. For we want students to speak knowledgeably, articulately, and with conviction. I have found that offering students a range of possibilities during a school term, from assigned topics, to shared topics, to independent topics, seems to satisfy. Included here might be:

- poetry recitations (either one's own or a published poem, either read or recited from memory)
- groups of students reciting a longer piece in turn, selections of dialogue from a book or play done as a skit (again either memorized or read)
- storytelling
- book talks (emphasizing theme or character, rather than merely restating plot)
- topical speeches based on student interest

The value of memorization cannot be understated. It is sometimes seen as sort of "old-fashioned." Yet I would suggest that memory is power, and that stronger students routinely have stronger memories. It is accepted fact that training memory improves memory (Caine and Caine 1994). Offering such experiences to students provides them with a chance to do something new and unusual and reap the benefits therein. That is why I generally prefer memorization of talks and presentations and rarely permit direct reading of text in a student talk.

As our final component of a successful public speaking experience, we return to our ongoing mantra of clear parameters for the task, with a representative rubric shared with students as the assignement is laid out for them. We also incorporate prompt and clear feedback immediately upon completion of the speech or presentation.

For a detailed view of an elaborate public speaking exercise for students that has proven quite valuable, let us now discuss chapter masters.

CHAPTER MASTERS

For many years as an adjunct professor in collegiate education programs I have found it beneficial for students to teach sample lessons in methods courses. They work in pairs, focus on an aspect of course interest, and plan and teach a variegated forty-five minute lesson, with handouts, visuals, and at least one small group activity. These partner presentations are always among the high points of the semester course. Students take the task seriously, use a detailed rubric, dress up a bit, and provide the rest of us with something novel and enjoyable most every time. Over the years approximately 80 percent of the students receive a grade in the A range for their partner presentations. They get written, immediate feedback from me, in addition to the completed assessment rubric, which is also translated into a letter grade. If it works with college graduate and undergraduate students, could it work with younger students as well? I can tell you that it does.

Two or three times per year when reading a longer novel, we will break into student partner pairs, and they will become chapter masters. Using a carefully designed rubric (see p. 76), selecting a specific chapter, and working within a twenty-minute time frame, our chapter masters produce terrific teaching/learning experiences for the class.

Students prepare well for this project knowing that they will receive a major grade. As with any assessment, the clearer the parameters, the better the student productivity. For their chapter masters assignment, students know that they are expected to provide clear and descriptive handouts, offer guiding questions, give a short plot and theme summary, and engage the class in a learning activity. The chapter masters experience is varied, often quite fun, and challenging for the students.

There is a social benefit as well. For the initial pairings students work with whomever they wish. This fosters student ownership and a relaxed classroom atmosphere. For additional pairings I elect to make the partner pairs. This allows an opportunity to socially integrate the class in a new way, putting students into cooperative ventures with one another and breaking down cliques and other barriers to classroom community. After initial and expected resistance, the students tend to work effectively together, and new social skills and attitudes are added to academic ones being attained.

We incorporate a student peer assessment component into the process, with two to four students using the rubric to assess their peers. They share the results with me immediately after the presentation, and I look for pat-

GREAT EXPECTATIONS CHAPTER MASTERS

Dyad _____ Chapter _____

	4	3	2	1
Knowledge of Chapter (guiding questions, facts, characters)				
Quality of Handout (appearance, information, mechanics)				
Creativity and Interest (energy, variety, originality)				
Class Learning (attentiveness, responsiveness)				

Total _____

Scoring: 4 = Requirements *exceptionally* fulfilled
3 = Requirements *capably* fulfilled
2 = Requirements *partially* fulfilled
1 = Requirements *minimally* fulfilled
0 = Requirements *not* fulfilled

Grading:
16 = 100   11 = 85
15 = 97   10 = 82
14 = 94   9 = 79
13 = 91   8 = 76
12 = 88   Below 8 = Redo

Comments:

Student Assessor _____

terns in considering the peer assessments' impact on the grade I will give. Usually we are close to concurrence in all areas, but not always. Then I must determine if I am off or if the student assessors are and how much to change my assessment, if at all. This peer assessment adds another element of interest for the student audience, as well as offer a few different roles for students to play in the process. What's more, it keeps me honest and relatively humble, while helping students (both audience and assessors) think critically, thus potentially raising their standards for their own upcoming presentations.

Although many kids are nervous before and during their presentations, afterward students feel proud that they have successfully stood up and communicated something of value to their peers and teacher. They tend to like doing this a great deal, often asking when we will do it again.

Because students can work together and are given ample time and shown clear criteria, the chapter masters experience usually results in good grades for them. And I am always delighted to learn new information or gain additional insight for a piece I am teaching, and to gain it from my own students' efforts. Chapter masters works well indeed.

AUTOBIOGRAPHIES

Effective assignments key into student reality. We are constantly seeking ways to make the curriculum current and vital. A major project that I have found to be an excellent vehicle for student writing and self-reflection is the production of autobiographies. By weaving experiences of this type into the school web we provide students with opportunities for creative expression that they may find uniquely valuable.

I enthusiastically introduce the project to the group with an overview on the importance of our human endeavor, the intrinsic meaning of each individual life, and a call to students to create something compelling and personal. The autobiography is to be approximately five typewritten pages, though it may be longer and often becomes so. It is to include a visually appealing cover, family photographs, and at least one quotation from anyone at all—distinguished personage, family member, the students themselves, or otherwise. (See p. 79.) I discourage them from simply cataloging their years chronologically, though they are free to approach the task virtually any way they choose. What I hope they will do is take advantage of the psychological opportunity presented and focus in some detail on seminal, defining aspects of their lives to date. Many of the students do just that, and to remarkable effect.

There is little reason to be afraid of what students might reveal, though the open-hearted teacher will likely be both surprised and upset by what is written. Even the timing of the assignment is important. If done too early in the year, students will not know me well enough to trust me with their innermost thoughts and feelings regarding central issues of their lives. Yet I must not wait until the last moment, either, or there will not be time to connect with students around what they have shared, should that be worthwhile. As it turns out, when assigning the project in the spring, I am amazed at what I receive in terms of both quality of effort and sincerity of feeling. As a result, I write full-page responses to many of the autobiographies in order to offer appropriate support and encouragement. Often, before turning over their papers, students actually require assurance that I alone will see their contents. Sometimes they even place a blank piece of paper over the cover page to guarantee privacy. And why?

These same students, who when first given the assignment routinely complain about the paucity of excitement and the lack of drama and meaning in their lives, go on to write incredible pieces. These pieces may be touching, troubling, appreciative, sensitive, dynamic, melancholy, and nearly all ultimately beautiful. As they begin to reflect on their experiences to date, themes appear, family members assume larger scope, events are reenacted, tragedies are delved into. Meaning is sought, and sometimes meaning is found.

Just this past year I learned of parental deaths, eating disorders, sibling rivalries, nasty divorces, substance issues, broken relationships, and all manner of healing. I have no ulterior interest in any of this; in fact it would be easier for me to have them write a book response or a canned essay. Yet I offer this assignment as a chance for them to grapple with deep issues that they most likely have not had the proper means to integrate previously. Not all will choose to do so. Not all have had serious doses of hardship. But many have, and many find the autobiography experience

Autobiography: Assessment Rubric

Δ   Ω

Student _____   Grade _____

Criteria	Fulfilled
Use thoughtful and descriptive **language**	4 3 2 1 0
Use **conventions** of standard written English: 1. spelling, punctuation, capitalization	4 3 2 1 0
2. grammar, usage, paragraphing	4 3 2 1 0
Organize text of writing in logical way	4 3 2 1 0
Title page and **subheadings**	4 3 2 1 0
Length: 3–5 pp. and attention to task	4 3 2 1 0

Scoring: 4 = Requirements *exceptionally* fulfilled
         3 = Requirements *capably* fulfilled
         2 = Requirements *partially* fulfilled
         1 = Requirements *minimally* fulfilled
         0 = Requirements *not* fulfilled

Grading:
24 = 100   18 = 88
23 = 98   17 = 84
22 = 96   16 = 80
21 = 94   15 = 76
20 = 92   Below 15 = Rewrite
19 = 90

Δ   Ω

liberating, as is clear from their papers. If even a handful of the students in the class emerge with a better understanding of what has happened to them and a truer picture of their own needs and motivations, then something powerful has occurred. They have changed for the better, perhaps. That makes for a potentially wonderful project.

The richness of the writing, the variety of responses to the task, the enjoyment apparent in much of the language, and the patterns of growth that emerge from the texts all point to the essential nature of the work students are doing and the attentiveness they bring to that work. This is an assignment that most of the students really get into. They surprise themselves with their level of commitment, routinely writing well beyond the ascribed length. And they often discover that their apparently routine lives are more complex and intriguing than they had thought. The cusomized covers of the papers are lovely to look at. Students are asking me almost immediately if I have read them and when they will get them back. They want that feedback, that recognition, that appreciation of their young and questing humanity. And in some ways it is better that it comes from a teacher than from a parent, especially in the adolescent years.

The use of the autobiography is effective on many levels, and I recommend it highly. For the writing of autobiographies not only improves students' writing and thinking abilities, it can even enhance the quality of their lives. *Voila.*

9

Parental Relations and Communication

It is obvious that the degree of involvement of parents/guardians (subsequently referred to as "parents") is a primary factor in the success or failure of children in school. All elements of assessment naturally concern parents, and for that reason a teacher's assessment practices ought to be clear, open, and available to parents.

Too often teachers see parents as a bother, a hassle, interfering, demanding, and so forth. We actually feel threatened, if we care to admit it. Ironically enough, parents often feel equally threatened.

The teacher is under siege for results and accountability, facing the daily demands of too many students, too many courses and classes, too many requirements, too much bureaucratic interference, undue time pressures, and on and on.

The parent, however, is equally beleaguered. And the parent of a struggling or unruly student is all the more distraught. Parents feel accountability, too, as well as a degree of public humiliation when their child is upsetting the status quo. It reflects directly on who they are and what they have failed at themselves. After all, failing as a parent is much worse than failing geometry.

Making the introductory phone call or coming into a school meeting with teachers, counselors, administrators, and other support personnel is not a fun thing for any parent. We must be absolutely certain not to judge too harshly, for the reasons for school difficulty are as varied as they are complex. It is quite possible that this particular parent has done everything he or she could have to this point, yet Suzy is still a troubled case in school.

It is even possible that this parent has done a better job than you or I could have done given the same variables. And it is certainly true that this parent cares, and likely cares a great deal.

We must recognize how we would feel if we were in that parent's shoes. And then we can build some rapport and develop a creative team approach in attempting to gradually turn the child's experience around.

Parents and teachers are equally at odds, and they are defensive at times because each is under definite pressure to produce positive results, no matter how challenging and often disadvantaged the individual is that we are required to deal with and finally educate.

SHARING INFORMATION

Back to school night or open house is an apt time to present one's assessment philosophy and techniques to parents. Follow-up mailings are also pertinent. The more parents know about the method of assessment, the more likely they are to understand and support it.

I begin with the premise that parents and teachers fundamentally wish for the same things for students—that they be happy *and* productive. When parents see that the game is positive and transparent, that the teacher truly wants each and every child to succeed in the classroom and that the assessment practices are meant to serve this end, it is likely that little confusion will occur and hence fewer problems will result. Developing collaborative relationships with parents promotes the success of their children in the classroom or school.

A word of caution here regarding the amount of information shared. Deluging homes with forms to sign, tests and homework to monitor nightly, and constant feedback leads to student and parent overload. It is not necessary that as a parent I sign off on every test my girls take, as they are generally strong and responsible students. I would rather have more description of what the teacher is trying to accomplish and fewer clerical tasks. And I do not need an endless supply of either. Periodic updates and accountability for students who are struggling is what we are looking for.

PROMPT RESPONSE

When a parent does contact us with a question or concern, we ought to get back in touch immediately and have the requisite information at hand.

When they contact the school, parents are usually seeking clarification and support for their own part of the home–school relationship. A quick response within twenty-four hours demonstrates our receptivity.

This short time frame will also provide us with an opportunity to immediately enlist the student as a participant in the process. For as part of our conversation we can suggest that the next day's homework be monitored, or a note signed, or whatever.

GETTING AND STAYING ON THE SAME SIDE

Initially the communication from home may be either defensive or aggressive (another form of defense, actually) when it is based on fear or ignorance. Calm and clear teacher explanation, along with a statement of concern for and belief in the student's potential for success will quickly allay most parental fears. Beginning a conference with academic positives and what the teacher enjoys in the student is a terrific method of breaking the ice and enlisting desirable parental attention. (Note: Dealing with truly wacky parents is more difficult and may ultimately prove impossible, but this is the rare exception. Most parents will be reached in time by a sensible, caring educator.)

More typical parental concern is to be welcomed, for it leads to a more cooperative situation. We are always attempting to present a united adult front when facing student problems, so that the young person sees that the adults are in harmony and desire the same results. A professional dialogue, either in person or by phone, should produce this unity and help the student to move in a specified direction, based on cooperative adult planning. Including the student in the discussion is essential but is best done after adults agree on a proper plan.

When an actual parent–student–teacher conference is called for, it is wise for the teacher to meet with just the parent prior to calling in the student. This enables the teacher and parent to get to know one another a bit, keep the student and parent from initially playing the counterproductive psychological games they likely play with one another when there is a problem, and balance the meeting so that there is no ganging up. This strategy also leads to the unified adult approach referred to previously.

It has been my experience that simply keeping an open mind and staying positive will often turn negative situations to positive ones. Just this year a parent called me with a concern about his underachieving son. "Mr. Crescent" was anxious and intent on his son improving his grades in my honors class. I could have easily dismissed Mr. Crescent as just another demanding honors parent with unrealistic expectations for his "gifted" son, whom we will call Adam. And the fact was that Adam did not strike me as a particularly talented writer, certainly not as talented as Mr. Crescent assumed him to be.

Yet far be it for me to determine any student's ultimate capacity or to in any way discourage any student or parent from holding to higher expectations. I resolved to hear the man out and try to come up with some simple, mutually agreeable plan to encourage this sophomore to improve his effort and achievement. As I listened I heard genuine concern, care, and hope on Mr. Crescent's part. Knowing that he was struggling with a serious, life-threatening illness made me that much more empathetic. I agreed to read a beginning of a screenplay Adam was writing and also to remind him to submit a piece for consideration for our literary magazine, of which I am the adviser. I also said that I would attempt to draw Adam out more in class discussions. His father could not have been more gracious and appreciative.

By the end of the year, when I called Mr. Crescent to invite him to our reception for parents of students with work in the literary magazine, as Adam's poem was accepted, we had a somewhat different student on our hands. Adam was more attentive, more confident, and pleased with his literary accomplishments. Perhaps he is on his way to something special. That little extra effort required of me was well worth it.

Seeing parents, even those far more demanding or difficult than the essentially reasonable Mr. Crescent, as equal associates in the educational process is a big step in establishing valuable home–school relations. Hear them out, while maintaining a calm, professional, and caring stance. Then patiently seek mutually acceptable solutions. This will go a long way in assisting us in achieving this most worthy goal of home–school collaboration.

10

The Secret We Share

I cannot overemphasize how essential it is to accept students where they are, assist them in moving forward, and structure grading strategies with these two thoughts in mind. Students should feel valued, understood, and supported in our classrooms. Their legitimate questions should be anticipated and answered in a reassuring manner. Each and every one ought to feel capable of success. Each and every one ought to feel better about him- or herself as a student and as a person as a result of being in our classrooms this year, so long as he or she made an honest academic effort and a decent commitment to his or her own learning.

As stated earlier, people are not simply competitive beings, nor are we simply cooperative beings. We are both, and at times we are neither. Classroom practices need to reflect this understanding of "human nature," whatever that term even means.

The teacher is the central character in a powerful play called *School*. Accept it or not, students are here against their will. Depending upon a host of variables, including the guiding philosophical framework of each individual school and classroom, the experience for students and teachers ranges from mostly rewarding, and even wonderful at times, all the way to godawful. In too many instances we continue to keep our students in a remarkably powerless condition where they are subjected to endless criticism, evaluation, and examination, and given virtually no choice in what they do during a given school day. It is an exercise in dull conformity all too much of the time. Simultaneously, the adults in authority claim in our long-since-shelved and dust-covered philosophy statements how our schools foster free expression, creativity, higher order thinking, and democractic attitudes. Oh, really?

Such situations, though darkly myopic and fiercely intransigent, are not altogether hopeless, however. Not for the person inclined to look at things a bit differently. All we have to do is occasionally remind ourselves of our own days as a child and a student, and then act accordingly, keeping foremost in mind what would be best for our own inner child. Then school may become somewhat reasonable, tolerable, manageable, and even a bit fun every now and then. And the learning will only accelerate as William Blake's "mind-forged manacles" are loosened and the energy expands.

My goal is that every student will leave my classroom at the end of the year both enjoying reading, writing, public speaking, and active listening more and becoming more capable doing them. This is one helluva goal. But what other goal should an English teacher have? It is not either/or. It is both/and. Do I ever achieve that goal? No. Not yet. But I get close in some years in some classes, and that is a beautiful thing.

This year I had two students come to me from another class in which they were failing miserably. Each was soon scoring in the 90s in my class, and one student went from receiving a grade of 55 in English before coming to my class to being named Outstanding Student in my class at the annual awards assembly. Last year I had a senior in my class who had done poorly in English his previous three years. He had a 93 average in his year with me and went on to college, where he will be a sophomore next year. The counselors know that they can place struggling students with me and get those kids a second chance at success. I like such a reputation.

A few of my colleagues, however, suspect I am simply an easy grader. But surely it is far more complicated than that. I suspect, no, I am certain, that some teaching practices in my district and elsewhere are routinely killing kids academically and spiritually. That is not why we are teachers. Our role is to inspire, to prod, to plead, to laugh, to shout, to nurture, to train up, to educate, to jump out of the window if necessary. Our job is our calling, and our calling is one that is noble and good. Anything that keeps our students from fulfilling their own unique, unknown, and quite possibly unlimited potentials is anathema to the task we do. Anything that we can do to make it easier for our students to succeed we must do. This does not mean success comes easily—far from it.

When I think of my students I picture their faces. Although they are adolescents ranging in age from fourteen to eighteen, their faces are young, bright, fresh, and open yet. They wish to succeed, though they do not always behave as though they do, or as though we would have them do. Adolescence is a time of pain, fear, loneliness, and desperate attempts to fit in—to a group, a class, a relationship, a family, a society, a future. Simultaneously it is a time of rebellion, of seeking difference, of experimentation and exuberance. These young people do not wish to simply fall into line, to become cogs in a great socioeconomic wheel grinding toward the imaginary joys of retirement. For many of them the only time is the present. Even the age of twenty seems distant and obscure.

And what do we give them, then? Challenge, certainly. But not artificially constructed obstacles designed to confuse and intimidate all but a few of the strongest and most fortunate. Honest endeavor, yes. But not tedium, not learning only for the sake of the next inevitable examination, not cramming narrow, isolated bits of information into brains begging for meaning. Expectations, of course. But not endless qualifiers constructed to prepare them for the next set of endless qualifiers.

Genuine education is not about getting one's ticket punched. It is not a game of survival, it is an—at times—exhausting dance of delight. And tests, yes. Tests of importance, necessary rites of passage, demonstrations of mastery, explorations of interest, enhancement of essential skills. And all done under a certain and fair amount of pressure and a natural elevation of intent. But not cut and paste, fill in the blanks, memorize, regurgitate, and expunge. Not guess-what-the-teacher-wants-me-to-say. Not do this boring deadly stuff only because you say I must do this boring deadly stuff. It has never been good or right for anyone. We can do better, and we ought to.

When I picture those expectant faces on the first day of school, those wryly laughing faces on the last day, or those anxious, curious, doubtful, blemished, intrigued, tired, receptive, inquisitive faces on any of a hundred other days, I feel a great responsibility. I want to help, not impress them. I want to hold their delicate minds and spirits in careful, strong hands, not thrash them with grading games of chance. I want to hear their viewpoints, their stories, as well as share my own. I want to spend time with them, not talk at them. I want to assist them, not evaluate them. I hope they may even come to love me in some way, as I am learning to love them, for who they are, not for where they come from or what they can do to make my experience a bit easier, or what they someday might amount to so that I could take some credit for their trip to the Ivy League and beyond.

These young people are somehow lent to me for a time, not to mold in some accepted image or turn into model citizens (lovely as such are), but to seek new and marvelous ways of being in this world together. And if I do my job effectively and take my charges seriously, each and every one, then I will see growth and learning in abundance. It does not come from me, however. And if it is not right for them it never works for long, it never sticks.

There is one other thing. We educators can never know for certain just what it is we have accomplished. These kids go on in school, and then out into the world, and most of them are never directly heard from again. We cannot even say with any confidence what has been achieved with them. Only they know that, and often not for many years after the fact. The secret is that most of what we truly teach is not even realized at the time by most of our students, if it is even ever surely known by us, their teachers.

We meet them, try to reach them, and let them go. That is all we can do. When done with love and their deeper interests firmly in our minds and hearts, it may just be enough.

Bibliography

Atwell, N. 1987. *In the Middle*. Portsmouth, N.H.: Heineman.

Bloom, B. 1957. *Taxonomy of Educational Objectives*. Boston: Houghton Mifflin.

Bloom, B. 1990. "Thoughts on the Bell Curve," *Educational Leadership,* 48(5): 17–20.

Caine, R. N., and G. Caine. 1994. *Making Connections: Teaching and the Human Brain*. Alexandria, Va.: Association for Supervision and Curriculum Development.

Caine, R. N., and G. Caine. 1997. *Education on the Edge of Possibiilty*. Alexandria, Va.: Association for Supervision and Curriculum Development

Daniels, H. 1994. *Literature Circles: Voices and Choice in the Student-Centered Classroom*. York, Maine: Steinhouse.

Glasser, W. 1985. *Control Theory in the Classroom*. New York: Harper and Row.

Glasser, W. 1990. *The Quality School*. New York: Harper and Row.

Goleman, D. 1995. *Emotional Intelligence: Why It Can Matter More Than IQ*. New York: Bantam.

Hannaford, C. 1995. *Smart Moves: Why Learning Is Not All in Your Head*. Arlington, Va.: Great Ocean Publishers.

Hirsch, E. D. 1987. *The Dictionary of Cultural Literacy*. New York: Random House.

Jensen, A. 1998. *Teaching with Brain in Mind*. Alexandria, Va.: Association for Supervision and Curriculum Development.

Kohn, A. 1990. *The Brighter Side of Human Nature: Altruism and Empathy in Everyday Life*. New York: Basic Books.

Kohn, A. 1993. *Punished by Rewards: The Trouble with Gold Stars, Incentive Plans and Other Bribes*. New York: Houghton Mifflin.

Landes, W. 1999. *The Wealth and Poverty of Nations: Why Some Are So Rich and Others So Poor*. New York: Houghton Mifflin.

Marzano, R. 2000. *Transforming Classroom Grading*. Alexandria, Va.: Association for Supervision and Curriculum Development.

Newman, M. 2000 (August 24). "Even With School Out, It's Work, Work, Work." *New York Times*, B5.

Parsons, L. 1990. *Response Journals*. Portsmounth, Maine: Heineman.

Raebeck, B. 1998. *Transforming Middle Schools: Guide to Whole School Change*. Lanham, Md.: Scarecrow Press.

Snyder, E., ed. 1963. *The Collected Works of William Blake*. New York: EP Dutton.

Sousa, D. 1998. *Teaching Manual for How the Brain Learns*. Thousand Oaks, Calif.: Corwin Press.

Sylwester, R. 1995. *A Celebration of Neurons: An Educator's Guide to the Human Brain*. Alexandria, Va.: Association of Supervision and Curriculum Development.

Uchitelle, L. 2000 (July 23). "Making Sense of a Stubborn Education Gap." *New York Times*, sec. 4, p.1.

United States Department of Education. 1997. *What Works: Research about Teaching and Learning*, 3rd ed. Pueblo, Colo.: Author.

Wessels, J., and Clyde Burkholz. 1996. *Rubrics and Other Tools for Teaching Quality*. North Mankato, Minn.: Ten Sigma.

Whitehead, A. N. 1929. *The Aims of Education and Other Essays*. New York: Macmillan.

Wiggins, G. 1993. *Assessing Student Performance: The Purpose and Limits of Student Testing*. San Francisco: Jossey-Bass.

Index

About the Author

Barry S. **Raebeck** has been an active proponent of educational transformation throughout his twenty-six years in the profession. With a B.A. in English from Wesleyan University, an M.S. in elementary education and reading from Long Island University, and a Ph.D. in educational leadership from the University of Virginia, Raebeck has served in virtually every capacity in public education—as a middle and high school teacher, pre-K–8 principal, director of curriculum, middle school principal, and even as interim superintendent of a district with a one-room elementary school. He continues to teach education courses at the collegiate level as well.

He has written numerous articles for journals such *as Kappan, Educational Leadership, Principal, Educational Digest,* and *Executive Educator.* His first book, *Transforming Middle Schools: Guide to Whole-School Change* (1998), is in its second edition with Scarecrow Press. It is based on his work as principal of the award-wining Thomas Harrison Middle School in Harrisonburg, Virginia.

Since 1987, Raebeck has provided presentations, workshops, and keynotes for school districts and professional organizations throughout the country on the topics of grading for success; student morale and motivation; middle-level education; and brain-compatible learning.

Currently an English teacher for the Southampton Public Schools in Southampton, New York, he is also an adjunct professor of education at Long Island University. He resides with his wife and three daughters in Wainscott, New York, and may be reached at (631) 591-4633; fax (631) 537-4278; e-mail: raebeck@optonline.com.